A
BLACK
GIRL
IN
ORANGE

finding strength through the struggle

A
BLACK
GIRL
IN
ORANGE

finding strength through the struggle

T.J.Vulcain

DEDICATION

Everything I do is for my favorite two. Z and B this one is dedicated to the both of you. Love you forever.

ACKNOWLEDGMENTS

I give all acknowledgement and praise to the most high. For it was he who pulled me out of the dark places and whispered in my ear when no one else thought that I possessed value. I was broken and decrepit but he restored my soul as promised. Even though I walked through the valley of the shadow of death, I feared no evil. I know undoubtedly that my heavenly father was with me yesterday, today, and will be forever more. The English language just does not possess the words to describe the gratitude that I feel for the almighty to think so highly of me, that he would save my life despite all of my wrongdoing. That being the case, I will forever serve in his kingdom. For if I know nothing else, I know without a shadow of a doubt that nothing is impossible when walking with him.

Special Thanks

Special thanks goes out to my sister. Girl I love you so much. You are beautiful on the inside and out. Thank you for helping me fine tune this project to its perfection. I truly appreciate you more than words can express. You mean the world to me.

A Letter to Myself

Dear Black Girl in Orange,

It's been a long time coming and congratulations are in order. Girl, I'm proud of you. You finally found the strength to look at yourself in the mirror. It was tough recovering from the trauma, wasn't it? So difficult, to the point that you wanted to abandon the old you completely.

I remember when you blocked it out, pretending as if it hadn't happened. It seemed to be the easiest coping strategy but eventually you realized that it wasn't healthy for you to continue to go that route. You are deserving of more than what's easy. You deserve healing. You deserve to tell your story.

I can recall times when you began to disassociate from her. That's how horrible you once were. The old you had the mindset of a criminal and the new you didn't want to be affiliated. You cringed each time that her vindictive and hypocritical character surfaced. You hated her mindset and her choices. Her selection in men and her recurrent pity parties made you want to separate from her even more.

She didn't appear anything like who you were aspiring to be, therefore you couldn't love her while in the process of improving yourself. Consequently, you decided that keeping the nasty version of yourself hidden was best. Acknowledging her was difficult because not only were you embarrassed in front of others, you also were embarrassed in front of yourself.

It took a long time for you to recognize that ignoring and suppressing her was damaging. Try being more gentle with her. Nurture her. Extend some grace to her. You deserve that.

Do you realize that it would have been impossible to evolve into who you are without her existence? She is and always will be a huge part of you. There's nothing to be ashamed about. She is you. Embrace it. Embrace her. This is doing the work. Affirm that all parts of your past were necessary and every voice that tries to tell you differently, confront them one by one.

The foster care institutions, juvenile justice facilities and prisons were only chiseling you. All the loneliness, the hurt and the betrayal, were for your own good. It's time for you to trust the process. You cannot claim that you are proud of who you are, yet regret who you once were. That's only going to create ambivalence within. It's necessary that you own her completely.

I won't say that I'm proud of who you once were but you never would have discovered second chances if life didn't break you. Every wall that stood in your way was an indicator for you to pivot. Nothing happened by chance. Your life happened on purpose. Embrace that.

Quit being hard on yourself. You've improved immensely. Remember to set some time aside to celebrate your progress. You are strong and you are resilient. You are valuable and you are loved beyond measure. You are chosen, therefore no weapon formed against you shall prosper. You are fearfully and wonderfully made. You deserve abundance, but it's going to require you to stop concealing. Your experiences are your testimony. No longer will you be inhibited by your past because all things are working for your good. It has always been you vs. you. Beautiful soul, It's time that you begin to think positively about everything that has happened to you and for you. Just remember, *"For as a man thinketh, so is he."*

-*Tee*

PREFACE

"Great! So, the ten thousand dollars was approved, love? Can you ring up another five thousand dollars in store gift cards? My father's company will need some extra gift cards for the holiday raffle." I paused for a second and checked her vibe as she worked. "Don't worry, if you need to call a manager for approval, I understand." I added confidently. Unbeknownst to her, I already knew that she didn't need anyone's approval. Especially since I played this same scheme a thousand times before, and it wasn't necessary.

"No, I don't need a manager's approval, it's no problem at all." My new cashier friend replied just as I knew she would. "I sure wish that I worked for your father's company." She added jokingly. I chuckled in response while keeping my eyes glued to the screen of the register.

After she finished scanning the additional gift cards, she instructed me to swipe my card again as I had before and I did so with ease. The cards that I was swiping didn't belong to me and neither did the other five that I had in my wallet on standby. I was prepared just in case this transaction wasn't approved.

I had no clue who the accounts belonged to and quite frankly I didn't care. My only concern was getting the gift cards activated with high value so that I could bring them to my fence, who would be waiting with cash on hand.

"*Ching!*" I thought, as I watched the register spit out my receipt. I tallied up my new total in my mind. So far today's total was fifteen grand in gift cards. A thousand dollars was on each card.

"*I wonder if I should try for twenty*" I thought. I wanted to get the most that I could get because there was a strong possibility that the bank would clip the card by the time I reached the next store.

Still pondering, I looked behind me and saw patrons growing impatient in line. Then, I looked over to the register beside me where my best friend was wrapping up a transaction. *"Let me not push it this time,"* I thought. *I have other credit cards and I can always go to another store and swipe fifteen grand more."* I reassured myself. The card limits this time around were hitting extremely high amounts therefore I was confident that I could easily obtain another fifteen thousand dollars if not more. Completely on grind mode, I made up my mind that I wasn't going home with anything less. There was no such thing as having enough.

As I strolled to the car, I was on an adrenaline high. I felt like I was on top of this world. I just made thousands of dollars in a matter of minutes and I was ready to go and do it all over again. *"This is so freaking easy! I'm going to be rich!"* I thought.

My best friend and her aunt, who had also been swiping cards, were already waiting inside of the car. Before I could properly close the car door, they began questioning me about how much I had gotten approved. Proud of my accomplishments, I gladly told them.

"How much did you all get?" I asked already knowing that it was less than what I had gotten. That was usually the norm. Bestie revealed that she purchased four thousand and her aunt confirmed that she got six.

"I think my cards are dead. I went through them all." my best friend announced. Instantly, I felt horrible. I dipped inside of my bag and passed her three of my gift cards and her aunt one.

"Thanks girly" she responded with a smile.

"We're like family" I replied as genuine as ever. I was happy to help. This was my circle, and we were in this together. There wasn't anything that I wouldn't do for them. I had a lot of love for them. Besides, I still had eleven thousand in gift cards left. Eleven and fifteen weren't that big of a difference anyways. Not to mention, I was about to hit the next store too.

"If I hit big at the next store, I'll look out for you two again." I assured them cheerfully.

"Thanks" they replied in unison.

After we were done with our jobs for the day, my bestie and I had plans to go out to the club. Once we sold our gift cards, we would head home to get dressed, real fly. She had a wonderful sense of style, so most likely she would choose outfits for the both of us and I couldn't wait. I didn't need anyone else. She was all that I needed as far as friendship was concerned. The two of us together were like two peas in a pod and I was grateful for her.

As we drove to the next location, I pulled my Gucci shades down over my eyes as the sun beamed brightly. I could feel the wind blowing through my fresh sew-in weave. The adrenaline rush flowing through my veins along with the expectation of our next hit, made me feel invincible. I loved everything about my life. I had thousands of dollars sitting in my apartment and a man who absolutely adored me. My son was happy, healthy and loved, plus I had the coolest friends that anyone could ask for. *"What else could I possibly need?"*

MDC BROOKLYN

"This must be a bad dream." I thought to myself, as I gazed around in disbelief at my surroundings. Everything around me felt surreal. I couldn't believe that I was confined to a jail cell. *"What is happening here?"* I suddenly didn't recognize my own life. Has that ever happened to you? Have you ever experienced everything around you becoming foreign right before your eyes?

Before I continue, please allow me to introduce myself. My name is T.J.Vulcain but you can call me Tee. I can be described as a cute, light skinned, black girl, who is blessed to be proportioned in all of the right places. Although I was born in the United States the origin of my heritage is an interesting mixture of Haitian and Jamaican.

I am proud to make known that I ascend from a bloodline of greatness. My family has done well for themselves; on both my fathers side and my mothers. My maternal grandfather was a veterinarian and my paternal Grandfather was mayor of a small town in Haiti. It would take too much of your time to speak about all of the great accomplishments of my family which is why I speak only of these two, but trust me, when I speak of greatness, that's truly what I mean.

Most people assume that because I am a product of successful stock, my life growing up had to be good. That is the furthest thing from the truth. In fact, my childhood was filled with boatloads of trauma and the negative memories significantly outweigh the positive. My parents did well for themselves financially but did not perform the best in terms of parenting me. As a result, I didn't grow up in a normal home setting. Many of my childhood years were spent living in a slew of institutions. I ended up being a ward of the foster care system and eventually aged out at eighteen to be left on my own. In the end, I became estranged from my entire family, which is a key factor as to why my life went in the direction that it did.

My childhood circumstances caused me to be feisty and this typically came as a surprise to most people because I'm short in height. My defense mechanisms were usually in overdrive but that wasn't the case on this day. Standing in shock, I was completely humbled and at a loss for words. I knew in my heart that I did not belong and I was upset at the way that I failed myself.

Sadness overtook me, as I thought about my reality. I wasn't the only one that was involved in those scams. Yet, I was the only one that was sitting inside of a holding cell in MDC Brooklyn. Something about the dynamics of that didn't feel fair to me. *"Why did I have to be the one to get caught?"* This bad luck of mine was beginning to get tiring. My life had officially become a complete and utter disaster.

My anxiety and simultaneous pity-party had been overtaking me since the case began. It was exhausting, to the point that I fell deep into a rabbit hole known as depression. Oh how disempowering it was to witness my own life taking a drastic turn for the worst without being able to change anything about it. I would go back and forth in a whirlwind of thoughts and end up with the same conclusion each time. I'd think to myself, *"Damn Tee, you really blew it this time."* I knew that I couldn't blame anyone but myself for my circumstances because when it all boiled down, it was a direct result of my poor choices.

I had the potential to do great things which is why I couldn't fathom how I allowed myself to stoop so low. This couldn't possibly be what God had called me to be. How could such an intelligent woman like myself end up in federal prison? Just the thought of myself being associated with prison life, filled me with involuntary shivers. *"Maybe, I'm not as smart as I thought I was."*

I have always been realist, and that will never change. As I begin to tell this story, allow me to first say that it may come off as brazen. I want to emphasize that I am in no way proud of any of the negative

2

things that I have done in my past and as I take you on this roller coaster ride, I want it to be clear that none of this should be interpreted as praise or bragging. My only intention here is to highlight my lessons as well as the transformation that I have been honored to experience from within.

Let's dive into the story, shall we? I stepped beyond the steel doors, with a feeling of despair washing over me. I was completely embarrassed, which is why I made it my business not to tell too many people that I had been indicted. Only those closest to me knew what I was facing.

Wide eyed I looked around for some indication of what was to come. It wasn't long before I was escorted to a special room and instructed to stand between two short concrete walls. I suppose the concrete partitions were supposed to provide some privacy. Yet, there was no privacy allowed in the instructions that followed.

"Strip of all your clothes." A female guard directed. Humiliation ran deep. Once I stripped all of my clothing, another directive followed.

"Squat down and cough." She ordered. I reluctantly did as I was told. I later learned the reasoning behind this procedure was to release anything that I could potentially be holding inside of my vagina. Once I was through, my personal belongings were collected in exchange for a khaki-colored uniform. The uniform was extremely oversized and wrinkled. The clothes didn't stink, but they had a slight stale stench to them, as if they had been in a closet for a few years. *What was the point of them asking my size if they were just going to give me whatever size they wanted?"* I thought to myself.

I was then issued a pair of navy-blue shoes that resembled Vans, except they were bad quality. After I was completely dressed, I looked down at myself in disbelief. I saw that I was completely disheveled, just as I imagined a person in jail would be. I hated everything about my new look.

Although I knew what was happening, I hadn't properly processed the consequences of my choices, or how my life would play out over the next few years. I didn't have an opportunity to. I hadn't been in my right mind since the moment that the NCIS agent called me on my cell phone to inform me that I was federally indicted. The months that followed seemed to speed by, like a plane on the runway. It may sound cliché, but I never imagined that one phone call could change my entire life.

Here I was, seven and a half months pregnant, waiting in a holding cell at MDC Brooklyn. I couldn't disagree more with the judge taking only a few months to decide that I should spend the next five years in prison. *"This can't be my life."* My thoughts began to wander.

I underwent a lengthy intake process which included being cleared by medical staff. Everything seemed much more complicated because of my pregnancy, and I was becoming annoyed. I saw men come in and get processed quickly. They all were escorted to their housing units, while I remained. My process seemed to drag.

After my strip search, the officer escorted me back to the holding cell. I made every attempt to sit on the cold metal bench but failed every time. It was extremely uncomfortable. I decided that it was more comforting to stand while I waited. The pressure that I felt from the baby positioned on my bladder combined with the hard steel bench was unbearable. I couldn't wait to lie down in a bed. Although I knew that bed would be no more than a prison cot, anything had to be better than the bench.

I'm not entirely sure how long I was left to wait in that holding cell. I estimate about two hours. I was tired and drained from all of the protocol and redundancy that I experienced during the intake process, and yearning to get some rest. Growing impatient, I asked an officer who was bypassing, if there was anything else that needed to be completed before I was moved. I didn't want to seem as if I was nagging but I was beginning to think that they forgot about me in the cell.

"No, you're just waiting to catch a ride with someone going your way." He informed me. This didn't register clearly in my mind.

"Excuse me? Catch a ride? Am I going in another car?" I asked, stricken with disappointment. He chuckled a bit, but not in a malicious or condescending way.

"No, no, the girl's unit is on the other side of the building." He explained nicely. This was reassuring for me to hear. My time in the holding cell would be finished soon. Looking around again, I saw the other officers joking around and playing. I became irritated by their jovial nature and happiness. None of them seemed to be doing anything of importance. *"Why couldn't one of them just take me now?"* My thoughts raged on. I was extremely cranky.

Adding to my irritability, was the urge to pee. I needed to go badly. The more that I looked at the toilet in the cell, the stronger the urge came. I just couldn't bring myself to use it. I couldn't allow anyone to see my behind tooted up in the air, nor would I allow myself to sit down on the seat. *"Obviously, they didn't intend for the experience to be pleasant,"* I reasoned.

Remaining quiet, I endured my surroundings gracefully. I had to prepare my mind because I knew that there was much more to come. I didn't ask any further questions and trust me that was extremely difficult for me. Taking a deep breath, I reminded myself that I was strong and could handle whatever was coming my way. Instead of focusing on what I couldn't change, I directed my focus to my unborn child. I began rubbing my stomach and humming quietly as my baby moved to the sound of my voice.

I lacked fear only because I wasn't fully present. I found it more comforting to deal with each moment as they passed. In hindsight, I realize that my thought process was clouded. Mentally, I couldn't handle thinking about much more than the moment that I was experiencing. I didn't realize that I was sitting in that cell completely traumatized.

A large part of me believed that I would end up okay. After spending a large part of my teenage life in group homes, and institutions, I knew that I could handle this too. *"This can't be too much different. What's the worst that can happen? Who's really going to antagonize a pregnant girl anyways?"*

Finally, an officer approached the holding cell and unlocked the door. I paused awkwardly expecting him to put handcuffs on me again, but he didn't. Instead, he invited me to walk alongside him and another female officer as they escorted me to the women's housing unit.

The walk was long and daunting. Everything was made of steel and concrete. I noticed that every so often we would bump into what I thought of as checkpoints. There was a steel door accompanied by a camera. The officers would have to press a button then look up directly into the camera for the door to pop open. It was all dull, gray, and depressing.

The escorting officers attempted to make small talk, but I was too focused on trying not to pee on myself. Eventually, they got the point and began speaking amongst one another. My thoughts were in overdrive as I had no interest in getting to know any of the officers.

I was happy when we finally arrived. Right away, I noticed that the female unit wasn't dull and depressing like the seemingly endless hallway that we walked through. There were pictures and decorations on the walls that were made from construction paper. The floors were extra glossy, as if they were freshly buffed. I made a mental note to be careful not to slip.

The unit overall was quiet and calm. That was far from what I imagined. I couldn't hear the television and I can recall thinking *"Wow we have to watch television silently?"* I couldn't understand why everyone was watching television with headphones on. I later learned that the television sound transmitted through a station on their individual radios. That made sense considering there were three televisions in one area. I made plans to buy a radio as soon as I could.

It didn't take long for me to become acquainted with the women on the unit and for that I was grateful. I was expecting the women to be big, buff and mean but they were the complete opposite. I was surprised that they quickly gravitated to me. It could've been because I was pregnant but overall, I noticed that outside of me, everyone seemed to be nice.

I was slightly wobbling, and I still had to pee badly. I asked the girls to point me in the direction of the bathroom and they did so without delay. I rushed over quickly. The separate stalls, in the corner of the big room, reminded me of school. When I exited the restroom, the ladies were still eager to assist me. Their kindness was a breath of fresh air after standing on my feet in that cell for hours.

One particular girl set me up by handing me a bed roll that included sheets and towels. Then she showed me to my assigned bed. It was odd to see the inmate and the officer on duty working together. It seemed as if the inmate was the person who assigned my bed. I committed to memory that she may have some power or ranking above the other inmates. I decided it would be wise to stay on her good side. She also handed me two rolls of toilet tissue.

"So, there are actually some decent human beings in jail." I spoke to myself, again. Here it was, I didn't know these people from a can of paint, yet they were making sure that I was good. One of the other inmates informed me that the two rolls that were issued to me, were expected to last a week.

"Use them slowly," she said half-jokingly. I guess they didn't realize that pregnant women used the bathroom more frequently. *"I guess I'll cross that bridge when I get there. Maybe the nice girl with the extra privileges will give me some extra."* I thought. I knew that if I needed some more tissue, I could talk my way to it. I was always skilled at talking my way through.

The welcome I received was appreciated. The women collectively gave me everything that I needed until commissary day came, which wasn't for another two weeks. I didn't need anything, and I didn't know one soul. This was how I learned that people who are from New York, look out for other New Yorkers. Luckily for me since I was from Brooklyn and we were in Brooklyn, I was covered. Although they said it was a New York thing, I'd like to think of it as God's favor.

I quickly learned that my name in the prison system wasn't nearly as important as my number. Of course, they didn't tell me that directly, but they may as well have because I couldn't do anything without that number. This number was required to make calls, to set up my email access and to send out postal mail. Basically anything essential to my stay required that number. I used this number so much that I was able to memorize it within the first day. I also figured out that the last three digits revealed to others which state my case originated from. I thought it was quite interesting. Who would have ever thought a number could become more relevant than one's name or story.

That amongst other things, I found to be intriguing. Another fascinating moment was when I discovered that we were counted. They referred to this as count time. At count time everyone was trained to scramble quickly and stand by their assigned beds. There were so many things I didn't understand, yet I never had an issue asking a question.

"Why do we have to stand at count?" I asked the woman in the bunk next to mine.

"That's how they confirm we are alive." She responded nonchalantly.

They counted numerous times throughout the day, however we were only expected to stand up for the four o' clock and the nine o'clock counts. On the weekends we had an additional stand up count at 10 a.m. I thought it was remarkable how well trained everyone was regarding the rules. It reminded me of how animals are trained.

Everything had a system, including communication. Cop outs were forms that were used for communication throughout the prison. For example, if I wanted to speak with the medical staff, I would have to write a cop out and place it in a designated slot. If I needed to meet with a case manager, it was the same course of action. Any request that was needed to be made to a prison administrator, such as the warden, was usually done through a cop out. Also, in the event that an inmate wanted to snitch on another inmate, they could do it anonymously via a cop out. *"How ironic"* I thought.

The visitation policy was one that I deemed unfair. There were too many rules. Not everyone was granted the right to visit. Visitors had to first be added to a visitation list. Anyone with a felony record, couldn't visit unless they were immediate family, and even that was monitored closely. The prison system utilized records such as our pre-sentencing reports to verify who our real family members were.

A pre-sentencing report (PSI) is a report that is generated just before one is sentenced. It is an extensive report that details your life, including but not limited to medical, educational, criminal records and family history. Every single inmate had one and they treated this like a bible. What one said didn't matter. If it wasn't documented on the PSI then it wasn't true. Therefore, whoever was listed as family is whom they granted visitation rights to. This eliminated inmates from adding "family" members to their visitation list.

Friends could also be added to the visitation list if they didn't have a criminal record. Potential visitors who weren't listed as family on the PSI, were required to fill out a background check form and mail it to the case manager in order to be cleared. Right away, I got with the program and made sure that my list was in the system.

Quickly, I recognized that the systems in place were calculated and intentional. It wasn't only about taking our freedom. This was a system designed to incarcerate us psychologically as well. I scrutinized everything closely and drew the conclusion that it was all deliberate. Unfortunately, I also learned that my awareness was irrelevant because I was still tricked into traps that I could see.

I learned a lot from the other inmates as well as the prison handbook. The women aided me in adjusting to a new normal. As I began to engage with some of them, I was taken aback by their stories. The number of years they were facing, and fighting was chilling. Ten years seemed to be the most popular sentence as a result of mandatory minimums. *"That's double my sentence."* I exclaimed in my mind.

Many of the women seemed content with that ten and I couldn't understand it. I learned all about the federal sentencing laws that held a common ten year mandatory minimum sentence. Many of the inmates seemed to settle and be grateful for it. Other women who were awaiting sentencing were also praying for that same ten years. From their perspective, ten years was better than fifty. Still, I had a hard time fathoming their concept of time. *"How could someone be content with losing ten years of their life?"* I wondered.

The ladies often reiterated that my time would fly by quickly. They told me how lucky I was to have a short sentence. They assured me that as soon as I was transferred into a real prison, my time would pass smoothly. I didn't believe them. None of them were in the same predicament as I was. I was the one that was about to give birth to a baby. Leaving my baby couldn't possibly be smooth or painless. I was convinced.

Although they were facing serious charges, they remained insanely brave. Some were fighting their charges and others were already sentenced. Not all who were sentenced were guilty. Many were guilty by association which is what the government refers to as conspiracy. Then there were others who served their sentences, were released, then returned to prison on probation violations. I found myself judging those women, from time to time. I would often think to myself, *"You gained your freedom, and came back here?"* I also found it strange that all classifications were housed together. Although my crime was non-violent, I was being housed with people who were considered to be dangerous criminals. We shared the space together yet we faced very different consequences.

I received the shock of my life when I learned that I only had three-hundred minutes to talk on the phone. It didn't matter how much money we had. Those minutes were expected to last for the entire month. *"Three-hundred minutes? What about us with children and families? I was already serving five years. Wasn't that enough separation from my family?"* If I evenly dispersed the three hundred minutes, then that would only equate to about ten minutes per day. This was the point where real frustration hit.

It was entirely a different world. From the limited phone time to limited commissary purchases. Everything was extremely controlled. Even the number of items we could order was limited. We had to create our own way of getting around it. Behind those walls you had to be innovative and utilize allies and trade. For example, if I wanted two cases of soda but was only permitted to purchase one, I would have to find someone else who wasn't purchasing soda so I could trade with them. I'm sure you can imagine how many trades went on on commissary day. Commissary was our lifeline and I was thankful that my husband was able to provide.

One of the most difficult parts of all was when I spoke to my three-year-old son on the phone. Towards the end of our conversations he would always say, "Mommy are you coming right back?" His words would send my heart into a frenzy. I hated that I had to lie to him. It was killing me inside, but what else could I say? Each time that the call was over, I was left feeling empty. *"What was the point of talking on the phone anyway?"*

GROWING PAINS

Daily, as my stomach grew, so did my attitude. I grew moody and uncomfortable. I remember calling my husband often only to complain about the stupidest things. If he came to visit me, I couldn't enjoy it because I was busy complaining about the last visit he missed. I was hurting, miserable and huge. It was disappointing that he was unable to relate to what I was going through. From this, I felt us begin to disconnect and I responded with anger and insult. We were a young married couple, and instead of growing closer, with each passing day, the walls between us seemed to push us further apart.

It wasn't all bad. Some visits were easier to bear than others. There were visits when we had a great time. We'd share many laughs and eat snacks from the vending machines. Naturally he was funny, so many times his jokes took away from the seriousness of what we were facing. My husband would rub my growing belly in an effort to feel our unborn baby move. There was no greater reward than for me to hold my son in my arms until he dozed off. I savored those moments. They reminded me of when I was free. The toughest part of all, was when those moments were over.

It was painful to watch my son cry out to me. On one particular occasion, he really didn't want to leave me. He forcefully grabbed my hand while looking up at me searching for confirmation.

"Mommy, come on." My baby said.

He wanted me to come home with him, having no idea that this place was my home for now. For such a small person he had a strong personality. Baby boy crawled beneath the chair that I was sitting in and locked his leg around it. His stance, if I wasn't leaving, he wouldn't be leaving either. The officers present tried their best to be understanding. They allowed us extra time to soothe him, but no amount of time would prove to be enough to separate a son from his mother.

My husband ended up having to peel my baby's tiny fingers from around the leg of the chair. It was then that I realized how intuitive and aware he was. Tears fell from my eyes as I witnessed my baby being carried over my husband's shoulder, kicking and screaming on his way out.

Back then, I couldn't understand that my husband was enduring his own share of pain as a result of my incarceration. I was too concerned about my own hurt. I can recall the day that I saw him sobbing at my sentencing hearing. He was the toughest person that I knew and to watch him cry was devastating. It was only after all of this transpiring, did I realize that he truly loved me. I reason that sometimes in love, it's necessary to withstand trials in order to build trust and resilience. We were young and the odds were against us. Still, I was committed to being optimistic about the future of our relationship.

Being loyal was my downfall, and I didn't realize it until much later. I was sentenced to five years in federal prison, due to my unwillingness to cooperate. I decided to remain loyal even if that meant leaving my husband, my three-year-old and the baby that I was about to give birth to, behind. I just couldn't see myself giving up my best friend and her family to the government. It would be like giving up my own family. I loved them too much.

Being estranged from my own family is why I remained true to the one that I was accepted into. I never truly felt like I had a real family until I connected with them. I knew that I couldn't afford to lose them which is why my sense of loyalty ran so deep. I refused to betray the people that I loved.

I also knew that my friend wasn't prepared to do this kind of time. She had two prior felony convictions, and I had none. I couldn't imagine how much time the feds would have given her. I rationalized that five years for me was better than some outrageous sentence for her. After considering all the facts, I decided that it was better to be a selfless sacrifice than to give up my best friend along with other members of her family.

The night after the emotional visit with my husband and son, I suffered from crying spells. No matter how optimistic I tried to be, I couldn't quite see the light at the end of the tunnel. I began to question whether I'd made the right decision. I wrestled mentally with what to do next. *"No, no I can't cooperate."* For every positive thought I was faced with one filled with doubt and despair. *"Would Bestie really help to raise my children like she promised? Who was really going to make sure that I was okay in here?"*

I found myself feeling lonely, uncomfortable, confused, and afraid as I laid quietly on my prison cot. I had no idea how I was going to be able to get through it all. It was a dreadful state to be in; to be unsure about a life altering decision that I made from my heart. Many nights were spent, toiling over these same thoughts. My problem was that I wanted to be a good person so badly that I forgot about myself.

It wasn't long before I began to adjust to my new reality. I quickly realized that I needed to become acclimated if I wanted to both eat and survive prison life. As expected, I was often hungry as a result of my pregnancy. The first thing that I learned to do was to prepare delicious meals by combining the kitchen food with commissary items. My favorite meal was referred to as a potato log. It consisted of crushed up potato chips that we would season and add boiling water to. This produced a thick batter. Afterwards, we would stuff that batter with meats, vegetables, and cheese. Upon completion, it resembled a long-stuffed log. Once cooked in the microwave for a few minutes, the cheese would slightly ooze out of the sides. It was impossible to tell that the outer layer wasn't real potatoes. Potato logs were absolutely delicious, and I quickly became an expert at making them.

Without many other activities to do at the facility, cooking became my specialty. I became so good at preparing meals that others would also ask me to prepare their food as well and I would. Besides, It wasn't like I had anything else to do. Not too bad for a newbie huh?

As my pregnancy progressed, I became increasingly uncomfortable. My ankles swelled immensely, and I gained a lot of weight quickly. Baby boy seemed to be growing at a rapid pace and it was becoming difficult for me to walk. Soon, I began to sleep for many hours throughout the day.

Recurring nightmares haunted me. I constantly feared that something bad would happen to me or my baby. Thoughts of not receiving proper medical care consumed me. I began to vividly imagine what it would be like to give birth while being incarcerated. *"Would they handcuff me during labor? Shackle me? Would my husband be able to witness the birth?"* I didn't have the answers to these important questions, and I needed to find out quickly. I was almost due.

In an effort to get my questions answered, I began to inquire with the case manager, as instructed by the other women. She informed me that I wouldn't be restrained during labor and I was so happy that I almost hugged her. My relief soon dissipated as she further explained that my husband would not be able to visit while I was at the hospital, due to protocol.

At that point, devastation fell over me. *"How did they expect me to give birth without my husband or family to support me? Alone?"* I thought to myself. This was cruel. I knew I had to advocate for myself. There was no way that I would be able to do this alone.

"Can I challenge that decision?" I asked boldly. If I was going to advocate for myself, I knew I would have to stand firm and show strength rather than fear.

"You can certainly try. Try speaking to the Warden on mainline but don't get your hopes up. The rules are usually the same for everyone." She advised.

Mainline is when the prison administration makes themselves accessible to the inmates for the purpose of addressing personal concerns. This usually took place once a week.

Although my conversation with the case manager remained at the forefront of my mind, I took my concerns with me into prayer. The following week during Mainline, I approached the warden. Carefully I presented my request. I added that I had a short sentence and that I was also newly married. I spoke from my heart when I explained how clueless and scared I was about the entire process. Even though many warned that it would be a complete waste of time, I was determined.

The warden listened patiently and he didn't interrupt me. When I was finished, he advised me to put my request on a cop out addressed to him. He said that he would make an exception just for me. I wanted to leap for joy but I was too big. I couldn't believe that it was so easy to get him to agree. Overcome with surprise, I had to make sure that I was hearing him correctly. I asked him to confirm what he was saying.

"It's never been done before, but I guess we can try it and see how it goes." he replied nonchalantly.

I must have thanked him about fifteen times. He went on to add that he didn't feel comfortable with my husband being present for the birth of the baby because he could imagine that it would be a hectic time. He would allow visitation immediately afterwards and up until I was discharged from the hospital. To say that I was overjoyed would be an understatement. I interpreted this small victory as an indication that although I was in a dark place, I still had the favor of God on my side.

Immediately, I called my husband and shared the good news and of course he was happy. For the entire day, I was cheesing so hard that my cheeks hurt. I recognized the blessings being bestowed upon me, even if they were happening under the most undesirable of circumstances. I definitely had something to celebrate and be thankful for.

I couldn't stop sharing my good news. I decided to share with another young pregnant woman who was being housed in the same unit. She was also from New York and I took a liking to her. She wasn't as far along in her pregnancy as I was, but she did reveal to me that there was a high possibility that she could give birth while being housed there. She hadn't been sentenced yet and was still fighting her case. As I shared my good news with her, I could see her eyes light up, as if I had given her hope.

"Do you think he'll allow my family to come to the hospital if I have my baby while I'm here?" she asked hopefully.

"If my birth goes smoothly, he just might. He's actually really nice." I replied.

"Girl, that's why we shouldn't listen to what people tell us. It's better to find things out for ourselves."

"For real" I agreed. I smiled real big for the entire night, on that hard ass cot.

LABOR PAINS

As I neared the end of my pregnancy, the medical department came to check on me frequently. They would periodically check to see if I was dilated, as well as draw blood for labs. It wasn't too bad for the most part. There was only one male doctor who made me feel uncomfortable.

Although he was accompanied by a female officer, it didn't make the matter any better. On one occasion when the female OBGYN wasn't present, I had no choice but to get examined by him. He was so rough that I almost told him to forget it. I wanted them to get someone else to check to see if I had dilated but I didn't have that option. Unfortunately in prison we did not have the luxury of opting for another doctor. Either you were seen or you weren't.

This same doctor also recommended that I induce my labor once I reached forty weeks of pregnancy. He believed that it was better to know when I was going to give birth rather than be surprised. He claimed that it was more convenient for the facility. I didn't care. I wanted my labor process to be as natural as possible, especially considering everything else in my life being so controlled. I knew that just two short days after giving birth, I would have no choice but to leave my baby and I was finally coming to terms with it. I didn't want to rush him out. I wanted him to let me know, when he was ready to make his entrance into the world.

The doctor didn't like my decision, but it was my right. I felt as if he were crossing a line. It wasn't his decision to make, and I was prepared to put up a fight. *"Why in the world should my baby's entrance into the world be at the convenience of the facility?"*

Doctor's advice aside, I went into natural labor two weeks after my due date. It happened on my cot. The pains began as faint back

18

pain in the middle of the night. Initially, I wasn't sure if it was time, so I didn't say anything right away. Instead I curled up in a fetal position.

I wanted to make sure that I was really in active labor before drawing attention to myself. As the officers were doing a routine 5 a.m. count in our dorm, one of the officers stopped by my bed to asked me if I was feeling pain. I admitted that I was and asked if I could take a shower. I didn't think that she would allow me to, because showers were off at that time, but she made an exception for me. I appreciated her compassion as it made a heap of difference.

As the day matured, I knew without a doubt that I was in active labor. I can recall trying to time my contractions, but I was easily distracted by everything happening around me. Although I had a son previously, I hadn't experienced natural labor. During my first birth, my labor had to be induced due to a leaking amniotic sac. Immediately afterwards I was given an epidural. Therefore, the sudden pains that were continuously getting stronger were relatively new to me. As I felt my stomach tighten with each contraction, I became uneasy.

Finally, around midday, I told the officer on duty that it was time for me to go to the hospital. My next course of action was to call my husband to inform him that I was in labor and would be leaving soon. The officer immediately made a call to another officer so that I could be escorted out. All of the women on the unit sent their prayers and well wishes, as I went on my way.

I couldn't help but feel afraid as I started on my way to the hospital. Thoughts ran wild inside of my head, *"I'm on my own in active labor. How am I supposed to trust people that I barely know?"* This was the first time that I felt sorry for myself. I couldn't even pray. I only rubbed my stomach and took a deep breath while doing what I was told.

Each time that a federal inmate is transported, there is a strict protocol enforced. Unfortunately for me there were no exceptions to the rules, even for a woman in labor. When I left the unit, I believed that I would be on my way to the hospital. Instead, I was taken to the infirmary. The officers were required to call the head doctor at home, in order to get proper authorization for me to leave the building. I was shocked. *"What if the baby were to come now?"* They didn't seem to be in a hurry.

The entire building was aware that I was overdue. I couldn't fathom why they couldn't have planned better. *"Maybe this is what comes with being incarcerated. Poor medical care."* I reasoned with myself. Nevertheless, I didn't have the strength to combat the ordeal that they were putting me through. I simply complied and followed their instructions. The only thing on my mind was making sure that my baby didn't come until I was in a hospital.

Within a few minutes we received clearance to move forward. An ambulance was finally called after a brief period of waiting. We walked to the opposite side of the building to meet them. The walk was about a half mile long. I stopped several times as the pain of contractions hit me. Halfway there, we were met by someone pushing a wheelchair to receive me. *"Gee, thanks."* Everything was so disorganized.

When I arrived on the other side of the building, I was released to the officers who would escort me to the hospital. Thankfully, I wasn't handcuffed, just as the case worker told me. Later on, I learned that a new law passed preventing women in federal custody from being handcuffed while in active labor. *"Thank God for that law."* I couldn't imagine having to be cuffed while enduring labor pains.

I believe that emotions are the key trigger of memories. If an experience didn't trigger an emotion then it could be easy to forget details. That may be the reason why I don't remember anything about the ride to the hospital except the officer snatching her hand away from me. I can recall like it happened yesterday. I was lying on the stretcher, twisting, and turning while my body was engulfed in pain. In a moment of desperation, I reached out to grab the officer's arm. I needed to squeeze something.

The female officer was insensitive. She was a white woman who appeared like a tomboy. When she snatched her arm away, the look on her face read *"Bitch, don't touch me."* That notion alone amplified my loneliness. For the remainder of the ride, I grabbed the bed rail and bit my bottom lip, hard. A tear escaped my eye and streamed down the side of my face, but I didn't let her see it. I didn't talk to the officers, and they didn't talk to me. That's one part of my experience that I will never forget. The blatant lack of empathy.

When I arrived at the hospital, I was plagued by stares. That was the day that I learned that pain doesn't take away from embarrassment. All that I could do was walk with my head down praying that I didn't see anyone I knew, after all not too many knew that I was in federal custody.

As the nurse checked me in, I became painfully aware of the stigma that came along with incarceration. I noticed that she directed most of her questions to the officer, who was able to answer most of them. The questions that she was unable to answer were then redirected to me. The nurse wasn't rude at all, yet unconsciously treated me similar to the staff at the institution, as a number.

Shortly after, I was brought into a room where the same nurse checked to see how far I was dilated. Imagine my disappointment when she told me that I was nowhere near ready, only a few centimeters. At that point she communicated to the officers that I wasn't yet ready to give birth. She explained that I needed to leave the hospital to return in a few hours. I became frustrated by her words. *"Leave and come back? Doesn't she see the predicament that I'm in?"*

The officers began to advocate for me. They explained that it was a tedious process to get me to the hospital. They also wanted me to stay while my labor progressed and tried to get that to happen, but the hospital refused. Soon I was on my way, just as quickly as I came. I found myself on my way back to MDC in active labor.

The pain increased significantly, along with my state of confusion. Tears streaked my face as we rode back to the prison.

21

"What did I do to deserve this?" I thought. I knew that I broke the law, but was the crime so bad that I deserved this kind of care? I was devastated.

I had to come to terms with enduring labor pains behind the walls of a federal institution. The officers were kind enough to bring a wheelchair upon arrival. This was a welcomed gesture. My body was in much pain and my thoughts were clouded with every scenario imaginable.

When I arrived to the unit, the women were shocked that I returned so soon. They were asking a bunch of questions in unison, "What happened? You're still pregnant." Exhausted, I made my way to my bunk. The ladies assisted me in any way that they could.

I endured the pain like a champion. Each time that a contraction hit, I would scrunch up my face and bite my bottom lip. To help ease the pain, I alternated between my bunk and hot showers. That was the only relief that I was able to find. I must have taken about fifteen showers that day.

Everyone recommended that I walk around, in order to speed up my labor. I made several attempts but the pain was unbearable. The more pain that I encountered was the more that thoughts of my reality hit. I would soon part ways with my newborn baby. Each time that I thought of the inevitable, I could feel my stomach churn. I longed for my husband to hold my hand and tell me that I was going to be ok. I needed a familiar voice with positive reassurance. Although I wanted to call home to hear his voice, I didn't because I knew that I needed to reserve my minutes for after the baby was born. Instead, I utilized the time to debate baby names and to talk to the other expectant mom.

As evening neared, my contractions started coming on more frequently. Suddenly, mid-conversation, I felt a big one. My body tensed up and a big gush of water followed. I gasped. There was so much water, enough for it to wet the bunk and the floor beneath me. Right away, the pains grew intense. I could barely speak. The woman who was assigned to the bunk next to me, immediately called out to an officer. I prayed that it would be an easy process this time around.

To my dismay, I had to repeat the same process all over again due to security protocol. I was escorted back to the infirmary, where they called the doctor at home, again. Once he gave the necessary approval, I was off. Again I was assigned two officers to escort me to the hospital once I got to R and D. By then, sitting or standing were no longer comfortable options. I found myself crawling on my hands and knees on the floor as the officers filled out paperwork. Normally, I would be cringing at the thought of touching the disgusting floor, but at that moment, I desperately wanted the pain to stop.

This time around, the officers were nice and to this day, I give thanks. There was a male and a female officer escorting me. The female officer was extremely supportive and the guy was cool. She coached and encouraged me the entire way. Her voice was gentle and soothing. Officers are trained not to touch inmates at all, but the female officer seemed to not mind that rule. She rubbed my back and reminded me to breathe as we rode along in the ambulance.

Once we arrived at the hospital, she began to advocate for me just like a loved one would. I was in no condition to help myself, yet God was mindful of me and sent someone who cared in my time of need. Very quickly I was assigned to a room.

As my labor progressed, I was no longer able to manage the pain on my own. I moved about wildly in the hospital bed, while crying hysterically. In an effort to bear the pain, I curled up into a fetal position with my backside in the air. My hospital gown hung loosely off of my body, which left me completely exposed for both officers to see.

The female officer noticed my distress and instructed her partner to wait outside of the room. When he exited, she came over to me rubbing my back again in efforts to soothe me. I cried for an epidural for what seemed like hours. When the epidural was finally administered, I was then able to relax a little. My mind became clearer and my thoughts more lucid.

With my mind clear, I became in tune with everything around me. As I laid in the hospital awaiting my baby's arrival, I began to feel the weight of my reality. A plethora of emotions came rushing to surface. When the physical pain subsided, the mental and emotional pain began to burst at the seams. I still don't know which pain hurt worse. My thoughts were continuously wandering to my unborn son. *"My baby and I have such a rough start. His childhood won't be anything like I imagined."* Warm tears streamed down my face, while I thought *"Girl, you really messed up this time."*

In an effort to escape my thoughts, I asked the officer if she could call my husband. I was ready for him to come to the hospital, as permitted by the warden. I didn't have much longer to deliver, and I wanted to make sure that he was downstairs when our baby arrived. The officer agreed, first calling the institution to verify that what I was saying was true. I was elated when she finally reached him, and he confirmed that he would soon be on his way. Hearing that, put a smile on my face. One thing I vowed to myself before entering prison was that I would always find something to smile about.

Feeling relieved, I dozed off to sleep. It couldn't have been more than a few minutes when hospital personnel bombarded my room, alarmed about the baby's heart rate. A nurse quickly placed an oxygen mask on my face, while another nurse urged me to shift to my side. They began to adjust the monitors on my stomach while observing the screen closely. Immediately I became concerned with all of the commotion going on around me.

"What's happening?" I asked in a panic. The room fell silent.

"What's going on?" I asked again. I could tell that they were stalling as many of them busied themselves around the room. Finally, after a period of silence the doctor announced to everyone in the room that he needed to perform a C-section. Panic and fear struck me. *"This isn't happening. A C-section?"* I panicked.

"No, please don't." I begged the doctor. I was shivering from fear as I spoke. I didn't want to endure a surgery alone. Numerous thoughts began to flood my mind. *"These people could remove my entire uterus, and no one would ever know. I don't trust them."* I heard many inhumane stories and it was hard to keep my mind from wandering.

"Why do I need a C-section?" I questioned, full with suspicion. My forehead creased.

"The baby's oxygen levels are dangerously low. You must sign a consent for us to begin." He informed me. I stared at him for a moment trying to read his face. I looked at all the nurses in the room as well. They all seemed genuinely worried.

"I need you to explain to me in detail exactly what you are seeing on the screen. Show me his oxygen levels" I demanded. The nurse complied by turning the monitor towards me and briefly explained what was on the screen.

"Miss, it's your choice, but if we don't get the baby out right now, he could die or have serious complications. We need to do this now. There's no time." The doctor interjected with force. His warning was all that I needed to sign the consent form. Once the consent form was signed, they immediately began treating me. One nurse was shaving my pubic hair as the others raced me into the operating room. I was there within seconds. I wished so badly that my husband or best friend could be present. I needed someone to advocate for me, in the instance that I couldn't advocate for myself. I found myself with my back against the wall. All I could do was trust God and believe that he would take care of me.

Sometime later, I realized that I was more numb than I was before. *"They must have given me more medication, but when?"* I thought. I couldn't feel anything. I spoke up, explaining that it felt as if a weight was sitting on my chest. My concerns fell on deaf ears, as the medical staff appeared annoyed by my constant concerns. They later reassured me that everything I was feeling was normal. The only thing that was soothing was the presence of the nice officer, who sat quietly in a corner of the room. I couldn't see anyone or anything else in the room, so I kept my eyes glued to her. I watched her eyes because the eyes never lie.

Within seconds, the medical staff informed me that I was being cut. Not long thereafter I began to feel my body slightly shift from side to side. *"They're probably being rough because I'm a prisoner."* I thought. Everything being done at that moment caused me to be suspicious. Thankfully, I felt nothing other than the tugging.

"There he is," The nice officer exclaimed. *"Ok, but why isn't he crying?"* I wondered. I desperately wanted to see him, but it was impossible due to the white sheet that was blocking my view.

"Is he ok?" I asked nervously.

No one responded. I looked over at the nice officer, but she too was focused on my baby. I tried to read her face for signs of distress. There were none. No one in the room seemed to be worried about me. I needed to hear a cry to be able to breathe properly again. I really needed my man. If he were present, he would have made sure that everything was ok.

Suddenly a squeaky loud cry filled the room. I closed my eyes and thanked God silently. *"We made it this far! My baby boy and I were okay."* A Nurse wrapped my new baby up in a hospital blanket, then brought him close to my cheek. It was a joyous moment. Instantly amnesia seeped in as I forgot all about what happened prior. All I wanted to do was soak in the moment. Taking a deep breath, I embedded his scent in my mind. I vowed to never forget it. His scent was fresh and he was perfect. I kissed him repeatedly. It didn't matter to me that he was still partially covered in white stuff. Though I was extremely tired, I was in awe. I could feel the love radiating between the two of us, in those few moments, we formed a bond.

I could hardly keep my eyes open as the medical staff stitched me. Periodically, I glanced over to check on my baby. He was tightly swaddled and sleeping soundly underneath a bright light. The last thing I can remember before I lost the battle of keeping my eyelids open was him being rolled out of the operating room.

"See you soon, little fella" I said softly as I drifted off to sleep.

BABY BOY

I didn't sleep for too long. When I woke up I was no longer numb and happy that I could feel my body again. Immediately I asked for my baby boy and shortly after, we were reunited. I tried to restrain myself from thinking of what was ahead for the two of us. Instead, I stood in gratitude for each waking moment, recording every second in my mind. Mentally, I captured every detail of my son, from his curly locs of hair to his tiny toenails. I noticed that he even had a little tooth.

My husband arrived at the hospital a short while later. I was happy to see him, but I didn't show it right away. I began to nag and complain instead.

"What took you so long?" I questioned. In response he mumbled something about him having a drink with his boys to celebrate his first child. After kissing me, he immediately went to meet our baby boy. I rolled my eyes out of habit.

"He's so white." My husband exclaimed, somewhat surprised.

I continued to nag. My next complaint was that he didn't wash his hands before handling the baby. In an effort to silence me, he washed his hands quickly. When he was finished, he picked the baby up again then held and rocked him for hours. It was odd to witness his softer side, as it didn't appear often. The officers allowed us privacy by turning their back and staying by the door. We drew the curtains closed to enjoy the intimacy of our new family.

My mind began to reflect on our beginning as a young, clueless couple. I realized that my husband and I hadn't shared many moments of intimacy. We didn't have a tight bond because we hadn't spent enough time together. I was way too busy chasing money.

"Should I share how I'm feeling with him?" I thought, as I watched him interact with our baby.

Prior to my incarceration, hubby and I experienced sex and spent time together but we weren't vulnerable with one another. I was too afraid of getting hurt. We rarely experienced high levels of intimacy. I thought about the way that I treated him. As I began to reflect, I realized that I didn't treat him nicely. I thought about my mistakes and I had many regrets. *"Should I apologize?"* After much thought, I chose not to share my thoughts. I didn't want to risk ruining the last of our time together.

"Are you sure you can handle this responsibility?" I asked as the two of us peered down at our son.

"Don't worry, I got this." He assured me. Then he added less confidently, "I don't have any other choice."

Our moment was disrupted as a nurse came in to take the baby for tests. I became annoyed each time that they came to take him. I knew that my time was short, so I didn't want him to leave the room ever.

One would think with the amount of pain I was experiencing from the C-section, I would appreciate the small breaks. Instead, they were a constant reminder that I would soon be separated from my son. I became obsessed with time, as if I could control it. Every couple of hours I anxiously checked the clock. I was on a count down and it was going by quickly. As time progressed my body filled with anxiety. I didn't have an inkling of how I was going to walk out of there leaving my baby.

Apart from my anxiety already being high, I was repeatedly trying to tell my husband that something was wrong with the baby's eyes. He was more concerned with naming the baby, than hearing me out. Knowing something was wrong drove my anxiety through the roof. I noticed that his eyes were getting caked up with a thin layer of phlegm. I would wipe them clean and then within a few hours more

29

phlegm would appear. I was alarmed because I knew that phlegm was an indicator of infection.

I asked a few nurses if they could look at what I was seeing, but none of them seemed to be taking my concerns seriously. One nurse said that she was coming right back but clocked out of work instead. I felt that they were ignoring me because I was a prisoner. I didn't have the freedom of going to the nurse's station to complain since I was bound to the room. Soon, baby and I both fell asleep,

When I woke up, I looked down to see the baby struggling to open his eyes, but they were stuck. There was a buildup of phlegm preventing him from opening his eyes entirely. Like what happens when one is experiencing pink eye. I wet his burping cloth and cleared his eyes quickly.

"My God, my poor baby could have an infection and these people won't take me seriously because I'm incarcerated. He could be going blind." I thought while studying my baby's face and condition. I couldn't do anything but lay back and pray. I refused to get upset or rowdy, after the favor that I was awarded from the warden.

My saving grace was a cool Italian nurse who I made friends with. She had a vested interest in me and my story. I loved that she had a high level of empathy for me and seemed to be a genuine person. I became excited when I noticed that she was on shift. When she made her rounds, I asked her to check on my son. She began examining him and noticed something was wrong quickly. She swiped over his forehead with a device and soon after he was rushed to the intensive care unit. The entire ordeal was nerve wracking.

A brief period passed before the medical staff explained that my baby had jaundice. His condition meant that he would be required to stay in the NICU under a light for a few days. They also explained that it was a good thing that this was caught early on. If left untreated jaundice could lead to brain damage. I praised God in that moment, he was always looking out for me and my family despite my circumstance.

30

I was overcome with gratitude when I received a positive update on the baby. He was progressing well in the NICU. Nevertheless, I was still a bit reluctant because him staying in the NICU meant less time spent with me. I couldn't accept that. I needed to bond with my baby, for as much time as I could, before returning to the institution.

Immediately I requested to go to the NICU but my request was denied because I needed to be escorted by an armed corrections officer. According to hospital policy, guns weren't permitted inside of the NICU. I began to pray in my mind, with all my might. I could not accept no for an answer.

"Can you please call the warden and see if he will make an exception for me?" I begged with my voice cracking. I knew that I was pushing the envelope, but it was worth a try.

"I can certainly try," the nice officer responded.

Her tone wasn't filled with much confidence, but I appreciated her efforts. It took a good while to get a response from the warden. Then, as soon as I was beginning to think that it was a lost cause, I got word that he approved my request. Gratitude and relief ran deep.

I couldn't believe that he did it for me again. The warden contacted the lieutenant on duty at the facility and ultimately gave permission to the officers stationed at the hospital. One was advised to stay at the entrance armed, while the other was directed to escort me inside the NICU unarmed. Additionally, he specifically granted me freedom to visit the NICU whenever I wanted, except during shift change for the officers. My level of gratitude flowed beyond what I can vocally express.

"Let's go." I screamed excitedly. I didn't have any time to waste.

The officers chuckled at my enthusiasm. I could tell that they took a liking to me. Soon we were off to the NICU. As I walked through the hallways of the hospital, I received many stares of judgment. Although I wasn't handcuffed, people somehow knew that I was incarcerated. Still, I held my head high, I had been given too

31

much favor not to. I was on my way to visit my baby. Nothing could steal my joy.

Getting over to the NICU was no easy task. It took about thirty minutes to get there with the help of my husband. The pain of the C-Section hadn't affected me until right then but I pushed through the pain like a champion. No matter how bad the pain intensified, I couldn't allow it to stop me.

Once I arrived at the NICU, I was overwhelmed with joy. It was rewarding to be able to feed, hold and nurture my son. I would whisper praise to God often, knowing that the miracle I held was greatly due to him.

Even though I had immense gratitude, anxiousness took over often. Each time that I saw a clock, my reality loomed over me. It was a constant reminder that my time was limited. I constantly had to shift my mind to focus more on the moment rather than think of the few hours that we had left together.

THE WORST DAY OF MY LIFE

"My God, today is the day that I leave my baby here." Thoughts began to flood my mind before I could fully open my eyes. My stomach churned and I became instantly gassy. Confusion, depression, hopelessness, and other emotions quickly overtook me. I didn't have much time to digest what was transpiring. Before I knew it, my thoughts were disrupted by a team of doctors entering my room.

The head doctor began to review the chart in his hands and then I heard him announce. "Mom is all set to be discharged today." The word discharged ignited a panic in my chest. *"Didn't they realize that I wasn't going home? I'm returning to a federal institution. I'm going to be separated from my newborn baby."* A slew of thoughts overwhelmed me. My body felt absent while my mind was moving at the speed of light. The hands on the clock were moving faster than normal as the moment I had been dreading for days, was quickly approaching.

A few hours later a nurse returned to my room with discharge papers. Once I signed, the correction officers began making transportation arrangements. Everything was moving quickly as everyone around me began making decisions on my behalf. I felt like a child without rights as they were enforcing protocols. It stung when I tried to ask questions and was overlooked.

I began to cry softly, "Please," I murmured. "I can't do it yet, I need some time." The two officers stopped what they were doing and immediately acknowledged me. For everyone else in the room, this process was normal, yet for me it was traumatic. That day, I experienced a wide variety of emotions in a short span of time. I thought that I would short circuit from overload.

I was never afraid to advocate for myself, so I did the only thing to do in that situation, speak up. It worked in my favor thus far. I simply had to pray and have faith that it would continue that way. The officers heard my plea and made a quick call to the facility. Favor was granted once again. The lieutenant on duty gave us the okay to stay for a few more hours only if the hospital agreed. The other stipulation was that the officers weren't allowed to exceed their shift time. With the extra support of my new nurse friend, I was permitted to stay.

"Make this time count," I spoke to myself as I made my way back to the NICU at a snail's pace. My husband was by my side the entire time, aiding me as much as he could. My body was showing strong indications that I needed another round of medication, but that wasn't important to me. I was on borrowed time, literally. It was just after eleven a.m., and I only had until three-thirty to visit with my baby.

Once I arrived at the NICU the hands on the clock seemed to be racing. Time was moving with the speed of light. It seemed as if I blinked twice, and it was almost time to go. In those last few minutes of time my baby boy's life began to flash before my very eyes. *"Could my husband handle this responsibility?"* I questioned from within. My best friend assured me that she would assist as much as she could, and I knew she would.

"I didn't turn her in to the feds, why wouldn't she help with my children?" My mind had taken on a conversation of its own. If there was anyone that I could trust, I knew it was her. That's just how we were for one another. I stared up at my husband and thought, *"Even if he folds, she never would."* She was family. Being estranged from my real family forced me to have to put all of my eggs into one very small basket.

"God will see us through," I reminded myself as the clock struck three-thirty.

"It's time to go," The officer spoke softly with her hand resting gently on my shoulder. No matter how hard I tried, It was impossible to prepare for that moment. I simply nodded my head in agreement, unable to speak. The NICU nurse carefully removed the baby from my arms allowing me the freedom to stand up from the chair. The room was mostly silent, and all eyes were fixed on me.

"I'm sorry hubby but it's time for you to say goodbye. Due to our security protocol, you will not be permitted to accompany us outside." The officer informed.

"No problem." Hubby agreed. The two of us avoided eye contact, while we kissed and said goodbye.

"Make sure you check on the baby," I reminded him as he prepared to leave.

"I'll be back later tonight." He assured me.

"We are going to wait about ten or fifteen minutes before departing." The officer announced once Hubby was gone.

"Ok so can I hold the baby, just one more time?" I asked the nurse, happy to have more time.

I needed to hug and kiss him once more before I left. When she handed him to me, I kissed his face repeatedly. My heart fluttered as he opened one eye, it seemed as if he was peeking to see who was kissing him. I took him snuggling closer to me as a sign that he approved of my kisses.

Ten additional minutes passed and the glance from the officer alerted me that it was time to go. I placed the baby in the arms of the nurse and prepared myself to leave. As we approached the door, the baby belted out a screeching cry. My heart shattered into a million pieces. There wasn't a dry eye in that room. I dropped my gaze trying my hardest not to cry too. The baby hadn't cried this loud or intensely, throughout our entire hospital stay. *"I wonder if he can sense our separation?"* I wondered quietly, as they pushed my wheelchair down the hallway.

In an effort to distract my mind from the cries of the baby and our separation, I began counting the tiles on the floor as we rolled along. It was only by the grace of God that I wasn't being dragged to the door kicking and screaming. I wanted to be graceful through this process and that I was. It didn't take very long to reach the front entrance of the hospital. Through the sliding doors I could see the sun beaming brightly.

The federal van was parked close by and ready to transport me back to the facility. To my surprise, I saw hubby sitting in my car outside. He wore a huge smile on his face and waved to me gingerly once our eyes met. His presence sent a warm feeling through my body, as I waved back to him. I wasn't sure if it was pure coincidence that he was there, or if he was being defiant in saying his goodbye's. Either way it gave me some sense of relief.

FACING REALITY

The officers assisted me as I climbed inside of the van. I noticed that there weren't any seat belts inside. Luckily, I wasn't handcuffed and had the ability to hold on during the twist and turns while riding. The pain that I was enduring was almost unbearable as I tried to keep as still as I could. Unfortunately, the potholes along NYC streets made it nearly impossible.

"What station would you like to listen to?" The officer driving asked in an attempt to cheer me up.

"Hot 97," I mumbled as I peered through the rusted gate on the windows.

My mind couldn't comprehend the words playing through the speakers. I was completely zoned out as we rode along. Not much time passed before we arrived back at the institution. The officers assisted me as much as they could, but the pain made the entire experience more intense. All that I could do was brace myself. The officers did everything within their scope of duty to aid me. Their acts of kindness and compassion will never be forgotten.

The sound of the steel doors closing behind us, as we moved inside, was a sound that I will never forget. A cold chill ran down my spine and I jumped with nervousness. Tears swelled in my eyes as I began to feel a great deal of self-pity. I was trying to be strong but was failing. I was then placed in a holding cell where the medical staff came to visit me. I don't recall much of the visit with them. I was physically in the cell but mentally I was on mars.

My mental absence seemed to happen often. I would find out for some time later that it was a natural response to trauma. My brain would automatically shut down as a protective measure. It felt a lot like brain fog. Although I was experiencing episodes of sadness, I never took the time to consider professional treatment such as therapy. In my mind therapy would present me as weak, and I couldn't have that.

As I think back to my very fragile emotional state, I wish that therapy would have been mandatory rather than optional, especially after just giving birth to a baby. Receiving mental and emotional support would have saved me from tons of situations I later experienced. My lack of awareness was dangerous.

WELCOME BACK

I was greeted with screams of congratulations, as I arrived back onto the unit. The ladies were genuinely excited to see me. They inquired about all of the details concerning my baby boy. I was most surprised to see that they made a card for me, which everyone signed. I treasured the warm welcome, especially after just being separated from my son.

"I knew you had a C-Section," an older woman exclaimed, as she helped me towards my bunk. I guess it was obvious by the way that I was walking. Her comment only triggered questions from many of the other ladies in the unit.

"What happened?" They questioned me in unison.

"Let her sit down first," The other pregnant woman spoke up for me. I chuckled to myself. It felt great to have a sense of community. Engaging in conversation with the women lifted the sadness that I felt prior to arriving back on the unit.

I believe that God strategically placed people along my journey to aid and assist me. I was thankful that he placed these ladies in my path in the nick of time. They were everything that I didn't know that I needed. Straight through the door, those ladies supported me. They encouraged me through difficult times. They were good to me. I came through the door judging them because of their crimes. Yet God used this experience to humble and teach me.

The host of people around me and the conversations weren't enough to eliminate the onsets of grief that came in waves. Those onsets were the worst at nighttime. I was overwhelmed by a deep feeling of depression during my first night back on the unit. I couldn't help but to think about my baby's light skinned face. I was adamant about maintaining the picture in my mind out of fear of forgetting.

The pain and longing for my son, caused me to be physically sick to my stomach. My mental rolodex flipped through millions of thoughts and scenarios.

"Was my husband at the hospital with the baby? Was he going to stay overnight? Has anyone else visited him since I left? How much longer would he be in the NICU?" I couldn't control my thinking. I tried to read in an effort to distract myself from intruding thoughts, but they were inevitable. It was also in those hours that I realized that I missed the opportunity to ask important questions concerning my son's health and wellbeing. Rest did not come easy as I spent most of the night zoning in and out of agony.

It didn't help that my current circumstance resulted in my faith wavering. The idea of surrendering control to God, made me uncomfortable. Instead of placing my trust and faith in him, I opted to allow my mind to spiral. I was literally driving myself mad. Mental debates continued within, to the point that my brain began to hurt. This would only trigger a crying spell that would last most of the night.

SETTLING IN

While enduring the separation from my son, I began to experience some of the harsh consequences of incarceration. Recognizing that I no longer had control or power was jarring. When I needed small favors, no one on the outside moved as quickly as I would have liked them to. I begged and pleaded for pictures of my newborn baby every single day. To my dismay, everyone who had access to him dragged their feet. Everyone from my husband, to my best friend and even members of my husband's family were promising me that they would print pictures and mail them. Each time that I got my hopes up, I would be left feeling crushed.

When I called, I would glue my ear to the phone as they gushed over my baby boy. The description alone wasn't satisfying enough. I wanted to lay eyes on him and see him for myself. Everyone who was able to see him said that he had the most mesmerizing gray eyes. They would also mention his tooth. This made my longing to see him even more intense.

A little over a month later, I finally received my first set of pictures. I was ecstatic. My baby was gorgeous. I couldn't stop staring at the photos. I took in every detail from his eyes, to his little chin, to his smile and even his tiny tooth that everyone loved speaking about. I was in awe of what God created through me. *"He has to be someone special."* I thought as I admired him through photographs.

The pictures were soothing. I noticed how much he already changed. Baby boy had more color and I was able to see those green eyes for the first time. My heart melted. I couldn't stop looking at him. He was everything I dreamed of.

Being proud of having another handsome son, I would show off his pictures and speak of him to anyone who would listen. This included both officers and inmates.Although I had received my long-awaited pictures, I still craved physical touch. Being incarcerated meant missing out on my baby's milestones. The pictures only gave me a glimpse into his life, and after a few days it was beginning to feel like a tease. I would have given anything to be present and do the things we normally take for granted. I longed to change his soiled diapers, rock him to sleep and learn his likes and dislikes.

There's an old saying that one isn't grateful for the moment until it's gone. I can confirm its truth. I found myself reminiscing on how he sucked from his bottle. *Was he anything like his big brother? Would he be just as feisty or would he be more reserved?* I wondered.

I also experienced moments of jealousy. Each time that I looked at a new picture, the thought of someone else enjoying all of those priceless moments loomed. A picture didn't have the ability to capture his first words. I wanted to cheer for him as he took his first steps. *"I am going to miss out on the most important years of his young life."* I thought to myself. This was monumental for me. I began to debate internally whether or not it was healthy for me to view pictures of him.

To make matters worse, the reality of me having no control was hitting harder as the days passed. I was unable to make my own basic life decisions. This hurt me to my core, but what hurt me even more is knowing that others now had the power to make decisions for my children, without my permission. That was the part that stung.

I hadn't taken the time to consider the after effects of incarceration. I was aware that prison meant relinquishing my freedom but the after effects of that were much deeper than I had initially realized. There were mental components of prison that I could never have prepared for, even if I trained like an Olympian.

Having to deal with my husband's family was a major one. My husband had a aunt whom I never particularly cared for. I knew her before my husband and I dated but my disdain for her began when he became my man. Everyone in the neighborhood used to warn me of her evil ways but I chose to give her the benefit of the doubt.

I can recall when my husband and I started dating, my best friend and her family disapproved strongly because of this same aunt. I'll refer to her as Aunt K. Aunt K was involved in witchcraft and was extremely manipulative and controlling. People rarely had anything nice to say about her.

Against friendly advice and my better judgment, I decided to date him anyway. I became acquainted with his family and for a while I believed their phony smiles. It wasn't long before I noticed an obsession between his aunt and my then boyfriend. She seemed offended by our budding closeness. She would often interfere in our relationship in an effort to break us up. She even went as far as trying to pick a physical fight with me once when I answered his phone. The straw that broke the camel's back was when I found out that he was hiding our marriage from her. I was offended by that. Eventually I decided to move forward being cordial to Aunt K, but from a distance.

I later discovered, on the day that I was released from the hospital and taken back to the facility, Aunt K. convinced my husband to allow her to accompany him on the way to the hospital. He agreed. The doctors were not yet ready to release my baby due to his eye infection. Following that recommendation, my husband and I had a conversation about it and we both agreed that the baby should stay at the hospital until his pediatrician agreed to release him. Somehow that quickly changed when he and his aunt arrived at the hospital. My baby ended up leaving the hospital against medical advice and he went home with Aunt K.

Of course I strongly disapproved however my concerns fell on deaf ears. Soon after, I found out that my husband was hardly present. He was spending more time in the streets than at her house with the kids. Unfortunately for me, that meant that Aunt K was now in charge and there wasn't anything that I could do about it.

Finding out that hubby had little involvement with raising our children infuriated me. I would scream and curse him out until I had no words left. I knew that we were young, still I didn't think that was a good enough excuse. I honestly believed that if his back were against the wall, then the man in him would emerge. Instead, he became weak and my complaints continued to fall on deaf ears.

To make matters worse each time that we talked, he was constantly in a drunken state and it was causing a lot of grief on my end. It wasn't until later on, that I realized that hubby was also suffering from my absence and his actions were his own coping mechanism. I was hurting so much that I only had the capacity to process my own pain.

The most aggravating part was having to play nice with his Aunt, whom he knew I didn't care for. It's a known fact that you catch more bees with honey, so I had to put on a brave face and deal with her. After all, she was my line of communication with my baby.

My husband's behavior drove me to question my choice in choosing him as my partner. Early in my sentence, I was able to see that he was severely lacking the leadership ability that we desperately needed for our family. *"How did I not pick up on this before electing him to be the head of my family?"* What a hard pill it was to swallow, knowing that I would have to sit back and watch things unfold for another four years.

TRANSITIONING TO DANBURY FCI

Although most of my thoughts were dedicated to my new baby. I was forced to think about other things as my circumstances began to change. It was time for me to move on. I always knew that the time would come but what I hadn't been prepared for, was the emotions that came along with it. Fear of the unknown consumed me. I would be soon transferred to a Women's Federal penitentiary located in Danbury, Connecticut.

MDC Brooklyn was a predominantly male occupied, high rise building, except they used one unit to temporarily house pretrial female inmates. This is why it wasn't possible for me to continue to do my time there. Initially they placed a transit hold on my travel as a result of me being far along in my pregnancy. They wanted me to give birth before transferring to Danbury. Then after having a c-section, they deemed it necessary to extend that hold in order to allow my body to heal. At about six weeks postpartum they considered me healed enough to travel. I had to quickly come to peace with the fact that I would soon be living in a real prison.

The women on the unit did their best to convince me that I would be much more comfortable at the new facility. None of their reassurance worked for me. I was sadder than ever before. I knew that the chances of me seeing my children would become slim once I arrived in Connecticut. *"How could I ever be comfortable in prison, when I have children in the world who need me?"* I thought to myself. No matter how hard I tried I couldn't imagine prison being comfortable.

On one random evening, I was called to pack up my belongings and that's how I knew the time finally arrived. This indicated that I would be amongst the next batch of transfers. Early the next morning around 5 a.m., the officers awakened a group of us, like thieves in the night. Mostly all of the inmates in the dorm remained asleep. The other pregnant woman along with others that I'd made friends with woke up to say their goodbyes. Then just like that, I was off to my new home. I was truly going to miss them.

On that day, I was extremely emotional. I hadn't realized how attached I had become to some of the women that were there. These women helped me through labor pains when I had no one else. These were women who had wiped my tears away and rubbed my back offering support despite them barely knowing me.

We shared food with one another and exchanged intimate stories. Some women were facing lengthy prison sentences and shared secrets that they shouldn't have told a soul. I didn't know if I would ever see them again and that made me most uneasy. This experience taught me early on that I was on this prison journey all alone and no matter how attached I became to others, when it was time to move, I would be moving on my own. As I moved on, I committed to keeping them in my prayers.

Danbury was like living in another world within this one. Immediately upon arrival, I was able to identify why everyone considered it to be more comfortable. At first glance, it resembled a small college campus that wasn't co-ed. However, there were some women who could easily pass for a man so that brought a sense of normality to the society. Contrary to what I imagined, Danbury wasn't as scary or intimidating as I had pictured.

I was surprised to see that there were all the luxuries of home life, without the freedom. There was the dining hall, a laundromat where inmates could send clothes to be washed, a church, computer rooms, an auditorium and a recreational building where exercise classes were conducted. The buildings connected with each other in a circular shape which left a large open space in the middle of it all. This was referred to as the compound.

There was even a beauty salon, yes you read right, a salon. The fee was a two-dollar voucher that was available for purchase at commissary. We also had the option to purchase relaxers and hair dye. I later learned that you had to pay the stylist an additional fee if you wanted the stylist to hook you up. Otherwise you would get something basic like a wash and blow dry or a roller set.

The small community was run solely by the inmates. The officers only supervised. There were thirteen housing units in which we lived. We were free to move about as long as it wasn't count time. There was much more freedom than I had anticipated. We weren't confined to a cell, and the officers didn't bother us much.

Movement on the compound was controlled during the day. During the morning hours from 8 a.m. to 4 p.m., we could only travel from one building to another during the first ten minutes of every hour. They would announce "open compound" on the loudspeaker. After the 4 p.m. count was clear, we were free to move around the entire prison, as we pleased, until the compound closed at 9 p.m.

After 9 p.m., the prison was considered locked down and we were then expected to stay inside of our assigned housing units. Still, we had the leisure of watching television, playing card games, and interacting with one another. There was usually one officer assigned to two housing units which left some units without an officer's station. They would do rounds hourly then once their rounds were completed, they would lock the main entrance of the unit and retreat to their office. We were then free to do as we pleased until it was time for count time.

As most would imagine, lesbianism was huge in prison. It seemed as if everyone was gay. This was relatively new to me. Of course, I knew what homosexuality was, but I had never witnessed it so up close and personal. I never had gay friends before, so I found these relationships intriguing. I previously heard stories from friends who experimented but never in a serious committed same sex relationship.

The prison relationships were a different ball game. These women would become violent if lines were crossed concerning their girlfriends. They were not playing at all. I quickly noticed that the majority of the women that were in relationships were catty and crafty.

Would you believe they even made homemade dildos? I never observed one being made, but I did overhear the process. The women would stuff a sanitary napkin inside of a rubber glove and viola a homemade sex toy was made. There wasn't a day that passed that I didn't learn some strange new thing. All of it was nuts yet amusing. One thing I can say is the women were determined. Where there was a will, they made a way. It's safe to say that sex was never lacking amongst the inmates even though they could receive an infraction for participating.

I quickly learned that I couldn't be friendly amongst the women. Being too friendly would only lead to one of two things. Either I would end up in a beef with someone's girlfriend or other women would assume that I was trying to become their girlfriend.

I found myself often proclaiming out loud "I'm not gay." This only led to a new problem, instead of respecting my boundaries they viewed me as a challenge and tried to turn me out. At first I was disgusted by them constantly coming on to me, however just like with everything else, I became accustomed to it as I loosened up.

MY NEW HOME

Initially when I arrived, I was assigned to unit two. Everyone on the unit seemed nice and welcoming upon my arrival. The women pitched in and gave me new toiletries and clothes to help me survive until I was able to shop for commissary the following day.

Thankfully, my husband put money on my books before I left MDC Brooklyn. I forewarned him that I wouldn't have anything when I arrived at Danbury if he didn't. I was informed that my property from MDC would take some weeks to arrive and I would have to purchase things to hold me over. The money that he sent automatically transferred with me and this allowed me to both make calls and purchase items from commissary right away.

Soon I discovered a bonus; my three hundred phone minutes also reset. This entire experience was instilling a spirit of gratitude that I never possessed before. I was overjoyed to have additional time to talk to my children and husband.

When I called to check on the baby, everything seemed to be fine. My husband and I were at odds, yet he was still around. He mentioned visiting soon and I couldn't be more grateful. *"Maybe we can still survive through this,"* I thought. During the call I also spoke to my three-year-old son. He seemed to be missing me badly.

"Mommy, when are you coming home?" he asked in his cute little raspy voice.

"Soon," I lied with tears beginning to well up in my eyes.

Four years didn't seem like soon enough, but I had to give him the reassurance that we would be together again. I hated when he asked that question and he did so most times that we spoke. It would be then that I'd quickly try to end the call, in an effort to remain sane.

On the unit we shared a tiny little cell and referred to our roommates as "Bunkie". There is no exaggeration when I use the word tiny. One person would have to completely leave the cell for the other person to enter.

My first Bunkie was an older woman serving a life sentence for murder. Despite her sentence and accused crime, I wasn't afraid of her. She was a mean woman who rarely smiled, which left no doubt in my mind that she fit the bill. She was hardened to the point that not many women on the unit liked her much but she didn't seem to mind.

There were a few times when I attempted to be nice to her, but her spirit still gave off evil. When she became angry and got into arguments, she used to say cruel things like threaten to stab or slice the person that she was arguing with. I never heard anyone speak like that before and often wondered if she was serious or only upset. Despite her flaws, I tried to love on her.

I know it may sound crazy to try and love the person I just described, but I have always believed that love heals so I did what I thought was necessary. I would say nice things to her and even share my commissary. Once I tried to hug her and she pushed me away forcefully. Still that didn't stop me from putting up an effort to get along with her.

I would constantly adjust my habits in order to soothe her complaints. If she didn't like something within our cell, I would do my best to meet her needs. No matter how far I bent for her, there wasn't ever anything that was good enough. She would simply find another reason to complain. Still I respected her because she was my elder.

When people on the unit would say mean things about her, I would defend her. It was a huge disappointment to me when I didn't make much progress with her. I have always believed that there has to be some amount of goodness in everyone. Sadly, I couldn't find hers because of the strong walls that she had built.

I later learned that each of my encounters were all a part of a divine plan. My bunkie taught me two valuable lessons. The lessons were cliché, yet valuable. It is impossible to force others to accept you no matter how genuine you may be and that everyone isn't meant to be your friend, especially in prison.

Another thing that intrigued me about prison was the infamous pill line. When pill line was called, it was a huge deal. At first, I was confused. I didn't understand because we were permitted to store medications that we needed inside of our lockers. Then I discovered that pill line was for the distribution of psychotropic medications or very strong pain medications.

Many of the women were abusing those meds. They were getting high and trying to escape. Many would smuggle the pills in their mouths, either under their tongues or in their throats. Buyers were lined up. It didn't matter how they needed to smuggle it. The medical staff would try to prevent it by crushing the pills up, but the inmates found a way around that also. It didn't stop anything. I imagine that the crushed pills only made it easier to snort. The drug trade in prison was major as these were the only drugs that inmates had access to. It was extremely rare to find street drugs in Danbury.

Television was another thing that was huge in prison. Before being in prison, I didn't realize how much people loved T.V. Thankfully, I've never been a television watcher, so it didn't affect me much. I considered my lack of interest in television a blessing since it was the source of many arguments and fights amongst inmates. There were typically three televisions; two of them were for English-speaking communities and one television was specifically for the Hispanic community.

Television was such a big deal that inmates would prepare for their favorite shows as if they were preparing for a date. Girlfriends would wear their best and cook a fancy meal, only to go inside of the TV room and watch a movie. Some women even had designated seats that everyone knew better than to sit in. Those women were mostly lifers, or women with longer sentences. Many would place a slip of paper with their name on it in a chair. This was their way of reserving their seats. If a hot movie was coming on, seats would be reserved as early as eight in the morning for a movie playing in the evening. I personally vowed to never be a part of the television drama. I was able to see that this was much bigger than television. Women in prison have little to no control over anything, so when the slightest opportunity for control presented itself, they became obsessed with it.

My saving grace came the day that they began to sell MP3 players on commissary. I have always loved music so for this I was happy. I asked my husband for the money to purchase one and he sent it quickly. We had the liberty to plug our MP3 players up to the computer and pay for songs through money that was on our accounts. I loved to purchase gospel. I would just zone out. I can recall sitting on my bunk, closing my eyes and escaping.. The MP3 player was one of the best things that happened to me there. We were living in a bizarre world and God knew that I needed that music to uplift my heart and mind. He used gospel music to keep me grounded in my faith.

Even though I worked hard to find peace, there were some things that shook me to my core. We often had random searches that were conducted due to suspicion alone. The officers were permitted to search our belongings as well as frisk us at any time. Some of the officers used this power in an effort to antagonize the inmates. What I hated most about these random searches was that female inmates were often patted down by male officers. I learned this, once one tried to frisk me.

"You're not supposed to touch me." I exclaimed, as a male officer began to randomly pat frisk me.

"Do you see all of these cameras around here? Do you think that I would be doing something that I'm not supposed to be doing?" He shot back. "Listen, my lieutenant instructed me to pat down everyone entering this unit and that includes you. Trust me, I don't want to do this just as much as you don't want me to, so please let's just get it over with." He added, seeming more aggravated than before.

As much as I wanted to protest, I held my tongue, knowing that I could never win. Although I complied, I was in distress. Feelings of confusion and humiliation overtook me. Unbeknownst to me, another inmate was observing the entire exchange.

"The male officers search us with the backs of their hands." she said in an effort to reassure me that things were okay this way. I guess she saw the look on my face. "You feel with your fingers. They can't really feel anything with the back of their hands" She went on.

What she stated made sense, but I was still uncomfortable. This was completely inappropriate. I never responded, instead I just stared back at her as if she had six heads.

"No one else views this as unethical?" I wondered from within. Each day it seemed more obvious that my basic rights as a human were insignificant within this prison. It was a shocking experience, being legally violated. I realized more and more that my previous institutionalization couldn't nearly compare to adult prison. These walls were filled with trauma and drama, and I was absorbing it all.

Being patted down by men was traumatizing for me but I couldn't speak on it because this was my new normal. I know that I couldn't have been the only one that felt this way. *"Why hasn't anyone spoken up?"* I wondered. I didn't want to appear as a rebel, so I remained silent. Still I couldn't understand how the inmates were compliant with what they knew was wrong. I silently longed for a change yet I lacked the courage to speak up. I speak of these incidents because I know it contributed to our mental dysfunction behind the wall.

AN ORANGE JUMPSUIT

The more that I immersed myself into prison life two things began to happen. The first was that I became distant from God. The second was that I became distant from the free world. I hadn't prayed in months, and it was obvious. My environment was beginning to harden me.

As I neglected my spiritual needs, I opted to keep myself busy. I figured that would allow time to pass faster. I wanted to avoid being caught up in my own head. I placed myself in every activity that I could find. I played racquetball, participated in step aerobics and other exercises, crocheted, and played board games. My favorite of all was playing cards.

Late night card games were a regular occurrence. Even the officer on duty approved. If we didn't bother him then he didn't bother us. The only stipulation was that we needed to be at our beds during count time. There wasn't an officer in the prison that didn't take count time seriously. Therefore we were well aware that we needed to be on our best behavior.

In an effort to continuously distract myself with fun. Blackjack became my game of choice. Prior to being incarcerated, my husband and I would double date with my bestie and her boyfriend on trips to Atlantic city. During those times I played often so I was familiar with the game.

It didn't take long before I became addicted to gambling. I didn't realize that I was betting more than I could afford to lose. I would stay up all night long playing. Wins were terrible for my ego. Being highly skilled at running my mouth, I would taunt the loser with smack talk. One evening, my trash talk went a little further than expected and I messed everything up.

I finally found myself on the right side of luck after a long losing streak. The woman that I was playing against happened to be a regular card player and her books were well padded. I'll call her Vee. Vee's family regularly sent money to her, in efforts to keep her comfortable. Therefore losing a few rounds wasn't a huge deal for her.

She and I developed a routine of playing cards together. We would lose and win back and forth. We even played spades together as partners against other women. The game took a drastic turn as I began to gloat hard. I rubbed my win in her face excessively. Being long overdue for a win. My ego took over.

I learned something about myself, through playing cards with Vee. I was secretly jealous of her. Though she never suspected it because I concealed it well. She had something that I didn't have and that was a family that she could count on. They would never waver, and she knew it. I admired her confidence in them. It was because of this that I paid close attention to her.

I needed the kind of support that she had, but I wasn't so lucky. I never thought that I would find myself jealous of another person yet I was. In hindsight, I learned that in situations like ours, what mattered most were the things that money couldn't buy, like family and real support.

"Wow, you're going to take care of me for my entire bid from just one game." I laughed with excitement.

My winning streak was continuous and so was my smack talk. I brought my group home behavior into prison without grasping that they were different scenarios. In prison too much talking could quickly land into a fight.

"You're not getting anything from me." She responded tired of my antagonistic rhetoric. The card game came to an abrupt halt as I took in her words. I was put on the spot.

"Excuse me? What did you say?" I asked, staring deep into her eyes. "You have no idea how I get down. I'll take your entire commissary bag when you go shopping" I challenged.

The unit lights were dim and most of the inmates were asleep as we were supposed to be on our bunks at that time. Our voices began to get loud. She laughed loudly, refusing to back down.

"You're so bad right? You don't need to wait until I shop at commissary. Just go ahead and take it now. I have a full commissary box and as a matter of fact it's unlocked." She added.

I was heated and feeling challenged. There was a small audience growing around us, leaving me no choice but to make a move.

"Okay," I replied.

I stood and moved swiftly towards her cell. Immediately she blocked me. Everything began moving at a rapid pace, as I put my hands on her. The two of us engaged in an outright fist fight. We were swinging on each other and landing hits like prized boxers. We went at it for a good while until the officer heard the commotion and ran out of his office towards us.

"Stop fighting, stop it now." he yelled out.

We were too deep into it. Neither of us complied with what he was saying. In my mind there was no use. We were already in a heap of trouble. We left the officer with no choice but to call in backup. He was such a cool officer who hated paperwork, so I know it pained him to do it.

Just as I started to get winded, I was forcefully slammed to the ground and handcuffed. Immediately a few buff men hauled us off to the SHU, also known as the special housing unit. Instantly I was filled with regret. Anxiety and nervousness overtook me. *"What in the world did I do?"* I questioned myself. The SHU can be described as a dark and depressing concrete place. There were tiny cells along a dimly lit corridor. The cells were complimented by ugly rusted bars.

I was stripped searched just as I described in the beginning when I arrived at MDC Brooklyn. Once the search was finished, I was handed a loose-fitting bright orange jumpsuit along with those cheap shoes that resembled vans. My commissary-purchased sweatsuit that I was wearing, along with my nike sneakers were placed in a clear garbage bag and confiscated.

I couldn't believe that I was expected to eat and sleep in that same one jumper. The orange jumpsuit made me feel like a real prisoner. I hated everything about it. I was then cuffed again through a small slot in the bars, to be escorted to another cell, where I would be staying. I noticed that all movement in the SHU required us being handcuffed.

As I was escorted along the faintly lit corridor, apprehension fell over me. The faces of those that I passed looked as if they served thirty years there. They looked hardened like gangsters. They appeared extremely comfortable and I noticed that most of them lacked grooming. Some had Bunkie's locked in with them. My mind began to imagine how uncomfortable that must be since their toilet was in the cell with them. There was no privacy whatsoever.

As I continued down the corridor, there were women standing by the bars of their cells only to observe me. My arrival seemed to be the highlight of the evening. Some of them tried to talk with me as I passed by. Some faces I knew from the compound, others I didn't. I didn't want to talk, my mind was slowly beginning to process where I was and what this meant for me. To say I was afraid, would be an understatement.

"Pretty girl, trust me, you're good here. I'm going to send you some soap, alright? " one of the women yelled out. *"How? Aren't you locked in too?"* I thought. I really was trying hard not to cry. I vowed not to show any emotions while in prison for fear of being taken advantage of. Instead, I walked quietly until I arrived at the cell where I would be staying. Every emotion filled me as I thought about losing the privilege of calling and checking on my sons. The rules in the

SHU were strict. Inmates were only allowed to make one call every thirty days. *"What in the world was I thinking? I have small children at home."*

Finally, I arrived to the cell that I would be staying in. I was relieved to find out that I didn't have a Bunkie. *"Oh good, at least I can take a dump in peace."* I thought to myself. That was my biggest reservation about being in the SHU. Well that along with the shower policy. We were only permitted to take three showers for the entire week. Before then, I never thought of showering as a privilege.

The mattresses were painfully uncomfortable and it was where we spent most of our time. They were paper thin, and hard to sleep on. I found myself unable to fall into a deep sleep because I could feel the sheet of metal beneath me. I would constantly shift from side to side, throughout the night, to avoid hip pain. It was then that I appreciated the mattresses out on the compound. I had no idea that it could get this bad.

The struggle was real. We were forced to spend twenty three hours of the day locked in and only one hour per day was dedicated to recreation. Majority of the time, I refused that hour because the officers often conducted rec early in the morning. When I did go, I was placed inside of an empty fenced cage that barely made it possible to access sunshine. I didn't see the point.

Then there was the disgusting food that was served. I refused many trays. There was no way that I was going to eat slop that resembled dog food. All that I could do was prepare myself for many hungry nights to come.

Just when I thought things couldn't get any worse, my fears were tested. Someone else came in and I had no choice but to share my cell. One day while the two of us were in the cell, my stomach began to hurt badly as a result of my needing to use the bathroom. I was curled over with pains and trying my best to hold it in. I stood straight up in a corner, for many hours, desperate for my stool not to leak out. I locked my butt cheeks tight but I knew that I didn't have much time.

"Just go," My new bunkie said casually as she laid on the top bunk, feet crossed and reading a magazine. "I promise no one cares, girl. Just flush each time you drop one, so that we don't have to smell it."

"I can't," I admitted, still standing in the corner.

I continued this way for an entire day until I couldn't stand it anymore. It was unbearable. Eventually I had no choice but to ignore my fears and go. It was such a relief, and honestly it wasn't as bad as I thought it would be. As time passed, I got used to it and ultimately became the nonchalant girl on the top bunk.

Another challenge for me was getting used to showering every other day. I was in my own head going ballistic. *"Oh Gosh, what if my period comes on? I need to at least wash my vagina."* The thought alone caused my stomach to churn.

One thought would trigger the next and before you knew it, I was having an entire conversation in my head. My bunkie on the other hand didn't have a care in the world. She would ask the guards for an extra sheet, hang it between the railings to block out as much as possible and then wash up like it was nothing.

The first time that I saw this, I was astonished. She would soap up from head to toe as if she were actually in the shower. The sink was all metal with a button that required us to keep pressing every thirty seconds to consistently get water flowing. She would fill up several Styrofoam cups to rinse and allow the excess water to stream down on the concrete floors and flow out of the cell. No one cared and the officers never complained. Ironically it was the natural order of things around here.

Of course, I resisted this idea, and my stubbornness cost me. I was smelly and I couldn't afford to wait another day to be cuffed and escorted to the shower. I became acclimated because I couldn't stand being stinky any longer. Before I knew it, I too was bathing in the sink just like my bunkie and many others.

My biggest stress of all in the SHU was when I began to think about the consequences for my infraction. I was fearful of how it was going to play out which resulted in an overload of anxiety. In prison when you're involved in a fight or another high severity, disciplinary infraction, you are required to attend a hearing with a disciplinary hearing officer, also known as the DHO. This officer acts similar to a judge. If he finds you guilty, he can impose time to be served in SHU. Most times he would impose additional punishment that he feels is befitting to the incident, such as loss in visitation, phone, email or commissary privileges. This could last from thirty days to one year.

The hearing wasn't nearly as bad as the wait to see DHO. Many people had to wait up to three weeks before they received a hearing. As if that wasn't bad enough, I learned that my waiting time didn't count towards my time that he would be sentencing me to.

In the end, I ended up being in solitary for a total of fifty-nine days with a loss of visitation and commissary privileges for six months. The DHO also took about twenty days of my good time which would ultimately affect my overall release date. I was saddened. That meant that I wouldn't be seeing my babies anytime soon.

At the end of my SHU time, I was handed the same clothing that I came in with. I noticed that my sweatsuit wasn't as fitted. I looked down at my hand and saw that I was pale. My hair was matted and my skin was ashy. As I walked back onto the compound, I could feel the sun beaming brightly and it hurt my eyes causing me to squint. As I strolled to my newly assigned housing unit, I saw that Vee was released as well. I could tell that she too had lost some weight. As she passed me I rolled my eyes hard. I'm surprised they didn't get stuck behind my head

She looked like she wanted to talk to me but I didn't give her the opportunity. I didn't want anything to do with her or gambling anymore. Besides, I had other things on my mind. I couldn't stop thinking about food. The first thing that I did when I arrived at my newly assigned housing unit was make a delicious potato log for myself which was followed by a long, hot shower.

MONEY ON MY MIND

I was able to bounce back from the bizarre SHU experience pretty quickly and began adapting to prison life more than ever. I traded in my free world mindset for one who was held captive by the system. This switch was completely unintentional. I began to conform to much of what was happening around me and it began to seep out in my behavioral patterns. A lot was changing in me and my marriage was becoming more rocky as time passed. My husband still wasn't as dependable as I thought he should be, yet I still wanted to believe that our marriage would stand the test of time.

Hubby was a certified street dude who had a lot of power in his community. I noticed that his position often demanded his loyalty. In the beginning of my sentence, I believed in my heart that he would return the same loyalty to me that he offered to the streets. I honored the loyalty that I had for my best friend and he witnessed it first hand. I thought that this would impress him on some level and in turn I had high hopes that because I stayed solid, he would also. Especially since she was his childhood friend. I was shocked when I discovered that he didn't have the same mindset as I did. This was a tough pill to swallow, as it became more and more evident that I chose the wrong man.

He grew more inconsistent with each passing day and it struck a chord in me. One thing that I knew for certain, was that if I continued to rely on him then I would soon be broke. Therefore strategizing and planning my next moves were imperative.

I was always independent and I was conditioned to handling my circumstances head on even if that meant breaking the law. I vowed that this narrative would be no different. Many times in my past, my downfall was my pride. I would prefer to break the law rather than simply ask for help.

Quickly I came to terms with my reality. I had no one else to rely on besides self. As a result of being estranged from my family, they had no knowledge of me being in prison. Therefore, I didn't have the luxury of asking them to help me. My friends would lend support when they could, but I was smart enough to know that no one was going to take on the responsibility of adding me to their monthly bills, and I didn't expect them to.

I thought long and hard about my next move and concluded that the money that I needed to survive through this would have to come from inside of the prison. Getting a job wouldn't merely suffice. The average monthly pay was only thirty-five to fifty dollars monthly and that would barely cover the cost of restitution.

Speaking of restitution, I was ordered to pay it back while serving my sentence. Many inmates with fraud charges endured this same challenge. FBOP would prorate the amount based on the amount of money that was received within a six-month basis. Whatever amount they decided was appropriate based on the formula, would automatically be deducted from my account.

With all the odds seemingly against me, I made a decision. If I was going to survive prison with little to no support, I had to return to hustling. I didn't want to be anyone's personal maid cleaning behind them or washing their clothes by hand. I needed a decent job and a side hustle. Stealing was all that I knew and up until the feds started watching me, I had been pretty good at it. I decided then that stealing was my best option.

This led to me landing a job in the kitchen. I was required to wake up at four-thirty every morning. I've never been a morning person but for this I didn't mind. Everyone knew that the kitchen was one sure way to eat in prison, literally and figuratively. Those that worked in the kitchen had access to foods that no one else on the compound had. I learned early on that if you have access to something that is hard to get, it was considered valuable. Value meant money and I needed it.

I ended up developing a plan. I would find a way to gain access to food that others wanted, and they could buy them from me. Working in the kitchen would also help me to pass time. It was a win-win situation; no brainer.

Unbeknownst to me, stealing from the kitchen wasn't as easy as I thought it would be. I assumed that my position would automatically allow me to gain access to certain foods. What I didn't know was that gaining access to valuable items required a certain etiquette.

There were unspoken rules known as prison politics. I later learned that everything behind the wall involved prison politics. To win, you first had to learn how to move. As I said before, the prison was mostly run by inmates. The officers would ask the inmates that were there the longest, for their opinion and advice on how things should be. These inmates were usually lifers or serving lengthy sentences. Rule number one, get in good with the inmates that ran things, or you wouldn't get far at all.

Once I observed this, I caught on quickly and eventually found my way. I got a job inside of the vegetable preparation department. This was a job that everyone on the compound wanted. The job entailed me being locked inside of a freezer room along with three other women, while preparing the vegetables and salads for the meal. Initially I was nervous at the thought of being locked in a freezer with other women with knives. My thoughts were scattered thinking of only the worst scenarios. *"What if someone becomes angry and starts stabbing?"* I quickly reeled in my thoughts as I thought of how easy it would be to execute my plan to make the money I desperately needed.

Shortly after landing the job, I got to work. I stole all of the onions, tomatoes, and peppers that I could. Each vegetable was worth one dollar and I was stealing boxes of them. I did this easily by passing the vegetables to women in other departments of the kitchen so that they too could receive a cut. I created a discrete system passing the vegetables through boxes.

This system kept me fed both financially and literally. No matter how suspicious the officers became, they could never prove it because I never had any vegetables on my person or in my cell. I knew that the secret to longevity was keeping my circle small while hustling and so I told only those who were involved in my scheme. I never even told my friends.

There were only two women that I sent the vegetables to on the compound. One was Asian and the other Hispanic. I didn't have to worry about them snitching because finding a link like me was hard. They would disperse the food amongst their community and in turn money was deposited on my books each month.

Are you able to recognize the patterns in my behavior? Once again, I fell into a cycle of stealing as means of survival. Did I lack integrity? I am not entirely sure. I honestly didn't see anything wrong with what I was doing. *"What harm is there in stealing a few vegetables from the government, when they stole my freedom from me?* I reasoned. I was creating my own morals. My values were distorted as a result of my environment. Choosing not to be accountable, I coerced myself into believing that since the government had taken my freedom away from me then my actions were justified. The truth of the matter is that I enjoyed getting something in exchange for nothing and I wasn't ready to change just yet.

LONELINESS

Although I fixed my money problems, I still wasn't happy. In fact, I was sad and lonely. I was surrounded by hundreds of women yet I felt isolated. Some days were lonelier than others. It didn't help that I lacked the comfort of the Holy Spirit, due to the void in my prayer life. This caused me to lack peace and solace.

I tried to become personable with some of the women who were incarcerated with me, but it didn't work because those women were also suffering as well. Everyone was hurting everyone. I too became a product of my environment. I used my words to be hurtful subconsciously trying to fit in.

Daily I witnessed hurt. The hurt wasn't always physical, sometimes it was mental or emotional. Witnessing such hurt was the reason why I didn't have many friends. I withdrew from being friendly due to the vulnerability that it came along with.

On the days when loneliness was unbearable, I would try to connect to my husband, only to run into yet another void. Most of the time he couldn't be reached. He became harder to reach with each passing day. I even went as far as calling Aunt K, who said that she too hadn't seen or heard from him in a few days.

My annoyance shifted to worry. *"He would never just dump my children on someone I didn't care for and skip town, would he?"* I started to think the worst. The situation with him just didn't sit right with me. I began calling everyone I knew hoping that they had heard from my husband. I came up empty most of the time.

On one occasion, I was able to reach him through my best friend. I knew for certain if she knew where he was then she would tell me. I also knew that if everyone else was lying about anything concerning him, she would be the one to tell me the truth. She had my back without a shadow of a doubt. We had been tight for many years so I knew that she was someone I could bet on and win.

My heart was beating anxiously as the phone rang in my ear. "Hello." I spoke quickly.

Her groggy voice told me that she was sleeping.

"Sorry to wake you." I apologized.

"It's cool girl, I miss you." she replied.

I hated small talk, so I got straight to the point.

"I haven't been able to reach my guy and Aunt K says that she hasn't seen him in days. Do you have any idea where he might be or how I might be able to reach him? I'm starting to become worried." I told her.

"Oh, I'm so happy that you called. He is on my couch right now. Hold on girl."

I was instantly relieved to know that he was okay. "Give me a second to wake him." She continued. I didn't say anything as I waited through my anxiousness.

"Hello." He answered dryly.

"Why is it so hard for me to reach you?" I started with him immediately. He rattled off a bunch of excuses.

"Why are you sleeping there?" I followed up.

"Aunt K's house is hot and there isn't any air conditioning. Our apartment is depressing Tee, I don't want to be there without you." He added.

"If your aunt's apartment is hot, why didn't you bring the children with you so that they could cool down also?" I shot back instantly.

"I just didn't want to bring all of that over here, I needed a second." He answered, cutting me short. I remained quiet for a while.

"I love you, and I really miss you. I want to see you soon." I finally responded hoping to shift the mood between us.

He began to say all of the right things once I took a softer approach. We talked for a while and then disconnected.

I noticed that he was vague and disconnected throughout our conversation. I began to wonder many things," *Is he in a relationship with someone else? Does he feel guilty about what he's doing while I'm here? What is preventing him from supporting me?"*

Vows before God, apparently didn't count for much. My heavy heart took me on a downward spiral. I was choosing a partner who wasn't choosing me in return. I witnessed other couples on visits and I would often compare. There were only a few husbands who fully supported their wives and I found myself quietly wishing that I had what they were blessed with.

I was honest enough with myself to know that I couldn't offer him all the things that he needed. I also knew that leaving him in the free world alone was a result of my wrong doing, but what about me? This was the first time that I saw a glimpse of his selfishness. Although he told me that he loved me during the conversation, I didn't feel it this time. Something just wasn't resonating for me. I didn't feel like he cared about me anymore.

I could feel our relationship dying. I could feel that we weren't going to make it. *"Where was his so-called loyalty?"* I knew that I placed myself in this situation, but then I thought about him also reaping the benefits of my prior actions. His entire wardrobe was funded by my schemes. Neither of us knew that it could become so serious. I was suffering from a lack of support and my husband was the greatest contributor.

HER

U pon arrival, she was the talk of the town. Nelly is what I'll call her. Everyone was inquiring. That's usually how it was when a new stud came through with swag. Many of the women would throw themselves at the studs as soon as they hit the compound. They would even have commissary care packages ready to give hoping that in return, the stud would become their girlfriend. In fact one of the easiest ways to be fed, if one was less fortunate in prison, was to turn into a stud. Many women would be eager to financially support them. I noticed that although Nelly seemed to like the attention, she was checking for me hard.

"What's up, pretty girl." I heard a familiar voice call out to me, in a deep southern twang. I looked up to confirm what I knew.

"What's going on Nelly?" I replied smiling.

"You're what's up Ms. beautiful. I've been thinking about you all day." She replied, grinning.

"You're something else Nelly." I said as I walked away blushing.

"One day." She replied ever so confidently.

Nelly was a young woman from the south, who recently arrived on the compound. She quickly became acquainted with counselors, officers and inmates. They all took a liking to her. I also took notice of her, becoming quite intrigued.

We lived in the same unit resulting in me seeing her frequently. I'd often hear her speaking about her case. Once I learned that the government sentenced her to over forty years, I felt a great deal of empathy for her. She often vented about her sentence and I didn't mind lending a listening ear. Through casual conversation, I couldn't help but take a liking to her. Her personality was different from any person that I ever met. She was funny and entertaining and this was refreshing for me especially since I hadn't laughed in months.

I found that she was able to temporarily take my mind off of my stress and I valued that. More and more, I found myself spending time with her. It was during these casual conversations that she began to throw hints. She had a big crush on me and it awakened feelings of euphoria within.

Nelly was on the heavier side yet shapley. I noticed that she always dressed neatly. Although she wasn't gorgeous, I found her to be attractive and that in itself made me a little uncomfortable. I didn't want to admit how I was feeling even though many others in the unit called me out on it. I noticed that Nelly seemed to be able to pull strings, which meant that she possessed power. Inmates and officers moved on her behalf simply because she knew how to move in prison. She always seemed to get what she wanted and I was fascinated by that. One evening during one of our casual conversations, she caught me completely off guard.

"Why don't you just try it and see if you like it? She asked, completely shifting from the original topic. I peered up at her in time to catch her licking her lips. My face turned beet red.

"Try what?" I pretended as if I didn't know what she was talking about.

"Try being with me" she replied while grabbing my chin in an effort to force me to look up at her.

"This girl is really touching my face and I'm sitting here and letting her do it." I was shocked at myself.

I liked her but I was ashamed. I had been approached by many other women upon arrival and I never gave any of them the time of day. Up until that point, I hadn't been phased.

"I'm not gay Nelly" I said moreso trying to convince myself.

"Yeah I know, but not for long" she replied confidently, as she walked away leaving me to ponder her words.

The following day, when I returned to the unit from work, I saw that my bed was moved. Nelly pulled a fast one. I was now her bunkie. *"What in the world?"* Curiosity took over and I needed answers. When I tried asking how this happened, all that she could do was double over in laughter. She refused to take me seriously. At that point, I marched towards the counselors office.

Once I was granted permission to enter, I got straight to the point. "Good afternoon, can you please tell me why my bed was moved?"

The counselor looked up at me grinning. "Didn't you want your bed moved?" he refuted.

Unbeknownst to me, Nelly was behind me. "Yeah she sure did" she said in her deep Southern twang.

Then she winked at the counselor. *"I can't believe this mess."* I stormed off without saying another word.

"I didn't want you in that room with that boy anymore" she said as she followed behind me, on my way out of the counselors office. I turned around shocked. My bunkie at the time was another stud that I was friends with. I figured out right then that Nelly had my bed moved out of jealousy.

Against my better judgment, I decided not to challenge the move. This is when a shift took place between us. The dynamics of our relationship quickly began to deviate from an innocent friendship into something involving a more sexual attraction.

Nelly would fill my head with compliments often and it felt good to hear. I hadn't had anyone desiring me in such a way, for a long time. She was taking my mind off of the void that I was feeling in regards to my husband. She was a much needed distraction.

Soon after, things began to advance between us as she began to be much more blatant with her sexual advances. Nelly would randomly whisper into my ears throughout the day, telling me how good she could make me feel if I simply just gave her a chance. "I *can't believe that I'm actually considering this. Who am I?"* I thought to myself. She definitely had a way with words.

To shorten a longer story, I ended up submitting to her advances. The entire experience was disappointing, to say the least. Thinking that I may have a different experience the next time, I tried again once more, however that experience was equally disappointing. To add to my disappointment. Nelly's endearing behavior ceased. She wasn't as nice to me and she began to ask me to buy items for her at commissary. I did as she asked the first time but then quickly became turned off once she continued asking.

Once Nelly saw that I wasn't going to allow her to use me, she quickly channeled her attention to a young white girl that was also living in our unit. The young girl then stopped talking to me and started buying everything for Nelly that she wanted. Then I heard her complimenting the young girl in the same way that she used to with me. She also moved her bunk closer to where the young girl was. To say that I was furious would be an understatement.

I wanted to put my hands on her and it wasn't because they were having a relationship. I was angry at the way Nelly embarrassed me and made a fool out of me. Feelings of shame consumed me. This entire ordeal caused me to be the topic of conversation on the compound. Everyone was gossiping about Nelly turning me out. I was overwhelmed and needed to talk to someone, so I jumped on the phone and vented to the only person that I could trust, my best friend. Unfortunately that didn't make me feel any better as she seemed to be more amused by the story than interested in soothing me.

For days I remained irate and tried to calm myself down however I was unsuccessful. One evening I became angry to an extent that I decided that I would fight Nelly. I didn't care about the consequences anymore. She didn't deserve to get away with humiliating me. I tied up my hair, put on my boots and waited for her, except Nelly was smart. She remained far away from me at all times. One time when she saw me walking towards her, she ran to the officers telling them that she felt threatened and was afraid. She went on to explain that she had a huge sentence that she was appealing and couldn't afford to go to SHU for fear of missed deadlines pertaining to her case. The officers kept an eye on her and I never got a chance to get to her.

As a result of displaced anger, I ended up having a fight with the white girl that she was dating. A heated argument escalated and I struck first. This lasted only a few seconds as everyone quickly got between us. Seconds later, I was faced down on the floor with a huge knee in my back. I could feel the officer's sweat rubbing on my skin as he handcuffed me. My cheek was pressing hard onto the tiles.

Moments later, I found myself sitting on a paper thin mattress while staring at the air through rusted bars. My new bunkie was taking a dump and I was pinching my nostrils closed while sporting a bright orange jumpsuit. *"What am I doing with my life? What in the world is happening to me? Am I Gay? Tee, you're losing yourself."* My thoughts raced. At that point, I was wishing that I never met Nelly.

ALL BY MYSELF

After enduring the exact same process in the SHU, eventually I was released with the same sanctions that I had received prior. This time around, my loss of visitation privileges drew me into a state of depression. I hadn't seen my sons in a long time and I now knew for sure that I wouldn't see them for the next six months. I was regretting my actions deeply. Most of my decisions only seemed to hurt me in the end. I wasn't smart enough to control my emotions and it cost me. Not only was I ashamed, I was also highly disappointed in myself.

Time seemed to slow down, and keeping busy wasn't helping much anymore. I was stressed to say the least. The only good part was that I was almost two years in. The wedge in my marriage grew vastly and that added to my sadness. It didn't help that each time that I spoke to my husband, he randomly asked if I was gay.

I knew that my best friend told him what I shared and it hurt me to know that we weren't as close anymore. When I asked him to send some money for me he replied sarcastically by asking me if I needed it to give to a girl. It hurt when he used that as an excuse not to send it. I decided not to confront my best friend, I just knew that I wouldn't share anything else with her that I didn't want him to know.

I completely transformed into a different person. I gradually stopped questioning everything and grew to accept things for what they were. There wasn't a guide or a manual, so I adjusted in the best way that I could. Within two years of time, I became accustomed to the consequences of prison life.

I completely conformed to the world around me and became much like the women whom I previously judged upon arrival. The compound became like home for me. The only exception was that my children, and friends weren't there. I became much more comfortable than I intended to. For example, when I was outside in the yard, I oddly yearned to be back in my cell. The feeling was like how you may feel when you're driving home from work. At that point, I was away from the free world for so long that all of my civilian experiences felt like distant memories. My new thoughts consisted mostly of prison news.

Many weeks would pass before I reached out to my children. I would become so busy that it would slip my mind. There were other times when I'd remember but convince myself that I was saving my phone minutes in order to avoid feeling guilty for not calling. Psyching myself out to justify my wrongdoing became a regular occurrence. This was a major coping mechanism for me.

There were many negative emotions attached to calling home. The conversations usually left me filled with much pain. I longed to be with my children but of course my circumstances didn't allow it. I was plagued by feelings of disappointment, confusion, and loneliness. My husband and I barely spoke and I hadn't seen him either as a result of my infractions.

After experiencing a level of sadness that was new to me, I decided to try my luck by approaching the Warden just as I did at MDC Brooklyn. My plan was to ask for a special visit. During my conversation, I referenced having a child while incarcerated and to my surprise it worked. The warden approved my request, despite my imposed sanctions. I immediately called home to set everything up. I was beyond excited that I would soon see my boys. This would also allow my husband and I the opportunity to speak in person and hopefully get on the right track.

I had my suspicions of cheating but I honestly didn't care. I just wanted to know that I could depend on him. Him sleeping with someone else was the least of my concerns. It was more important for me to know that I still had a family. I wanted to look into his eyes to see if I still had his heart. I commended him for holding the kids down this far, especially considering that my first child wasn't biologically his, but I still needed to know what was happening between us.

When visitation day arrived, I was bursting with excitement. I made sure that my uniform was freshly ironed from the night before. I put on makeup and even had my hair freshly braided. Once I was ready, I sat in anticipation of greeting my family. Then, after three hours passed, I became nervous. I hadn't heard my name called over the loudspeaker. I feared the worst. *"Did he get into an accident?"* I thought.

I began to call repeatedly but there was no answer. Then, I randomly checked my email as a last resort and there it was. There was an email from my best friend. She told me that my husband was not going to make it. I stared at the screen before me for ten whole minutes, unable to comprehend what I read. My shoulders slumped down towards the ground.

To say that I was devastated would be an understatement. She didn't give me any excuse as to why. Just a short, vague message that left me in a state of confusion. My friends on the compound were continuously asking when he was going to be arriving. I bragged about this visit for days and they were living through my excitement as well. I felt stupid.

For my own emotional protection, I didn't ask for any more visits for a while. I also stopped calling home as much. I didn't want to lose my mind by constantly being let down. My detachment was solely about self-preservation. It's why I believe I was able to preserve my mental state. I knew that I had still had some years to get through. I had to be honest with myself. At this point, my reality contained more clarity than a crystal. I was in this thing all by myself.

A BOMB DROP

Time is what allowed me to find peace with my prison sentence. I no longer cared about who knew about my incarceration or how they felt about it. Releasing unwanted stress allowed my time to flow smoothly. I no longer made plans because plans came along with a tremendous amount of anxiety. I lived only for the day that I was in.

My life consisted of working in the kitchen, aerobics class, listening to music, reading, and hanging out with some of the messiest women on the compound. I didn't take anything too seriously and I was happy to finally settle in to do my time. As long as I wasn't losing good days, that meant that my release date was approaching. My number one priority was staying clear of drama.

I didn't use the phone every day, but I engaged with my friends through email. This was my way of keeping up with the events happening on the outside. Email wasn't as stressful as the phone or as many called it *"The Painbox."* It was also much cheaper.

Most times emails were pleasant, except for the day that I learned of my friend's husband being murdered. I'll call my friend Dee. I sat in a state of shock after reading her email, having no idea how to respond to such a tragic event.

I wanted to be there for her badly, but I couldn't. Her husband wasn't a family member, so I wouldn't be able to attend the funeral. I couldn't imagine the pain that she was feeling and I felt bad for her. Right away, I contacted my best friend. The three of us were always real tight. I wanted to figure out a plan to support her even though I couldn't be present.

Oddly enough, my best friend seemed reluctant to support Dee. This was alarming to me because we always supported one another. She responded to my email by saying that she wasn't certain that she would attend the funeral because they weren't on the best of terms. *"Her husband was just killed. What do you mean you aren't sure about attending the funeral?"*

I was aware that they had their differences, however I never thought that those differences would stand in the way in a time like this. This moment forced me to realize that the beef between them may be more serious than I originally thought. The only thing left for me to do was to support my friend with prayer and kind words.

Let's fast forward to a few months later. I received another email from Dee. In that email, she stated that she had something important to tell me and that I should be sitting down when I read it. I quickly replied, eager to know what it was. She seemed to be beating around the bush as the next few emails reiterated that I needed to relax and stay calm as possible. This same pattern continued for the next few days, until early one morning. I checked my email, and there it was.

It was as if a bomb imploded in my face when I read the words on the screen. My best friend and my husband were sleeping together and they began seeing one another, three months after my incarceration. I stared at the screen with a blank expression on my face. I could feel heat rising from my head as I began to sweat.

Tears began to soak the neck of my shirt. I was completely distraught. One of the ladies in the computer room thought it necessary to walk me to my unit. Everyone on the compound assumed that someone in my family died. It sure felt that way. The two of them were my entire world. I put all my faith and trust into them. I couldn't believe it. It took a few days for me to process the news. When I gained enough courage, I called Dee. I needed to know if she had real evidence of what she was saying or if this was hearsay.

"Hello." The mounting pain was evident in my voice.

"Hey Tee, how are you?" she replied. I didn't really want to have small talk. I wanted to get down to the nitty gritty.

"I'm okay." I wanted to talk about the email. "How do you know it's true?" I asked carefully.

"I'm sorry but I had to tell you. I couldn't stomach it anymore Tee. She and I haven't seen eye to eye in some time and this situation is the reason behind it. Everyone has been talking about them. I also had my suspicions and I asked her straight up. That's when she admitted to me that they were sleeping together." Tears stung my eyes as I heard her speak. *"The same woman that I refused to snitch on is sleeping with my husband and I'm here in prison because I was protecting her."* My thoughts rang loudly. I couldn't believe my ears.

"I couldn't hide it anymore girl. Nobody wanted to tell you. She had the nerve to post a picture of you, on Facebook, for your birthday. The caption read 'I wish you were home.' That was the last straw. Those words disgusted me because I knew that they weren't true. After my husband was murdered, I look at life differently. It's shorter than we think Tee. I thought you needed to know" Dee explained.

I drank her words. They felt like poison in my stomach. Betrayal was a bitter experience. Still, I felt as if I needed more confirmation. I ended my call with her and went on to call a few other mutual friends. They each confirmed the same thing. Everyone knew.

"How could you withhold this from me?" I roared through the phone at one of my friends. "You met her through me!" I cried. "Your loyalty should be to me."

"Listen, you can't be upset with me. Tee, you have called your best friend early in the morning, looking for your husband and he's sleeping at her house. You're not dumb, you shouldn't need anyone to tell you anything." She roared back at me.

I swallowed those words hard. It was definitely something to think about. I hung up quickly, afraid to hear anything else that would upset me any further.

The contentment that I recently gained, immediately dispersed. It was replaced with deep depression. The questions that I had been plagued by all of this time were finally answered. I was dedicated to sticking beside the very same person who was trying to steamroll over me. My perspective was clearer than ever. I sacrificed my life, only to be betrayed.

My mind began to wonder as I thought about a conversation between my oldest son and I. During this conversation he asked if my bestie's son was his cousin or his stepbrother. I always viewed my bestie as my sister, so I assured him that they were cousins. At that time, I didn't realize why he was confused about that. I instantly became sick to my stomach, as I visualized what was happening in my children's presence.

"How could they be so grimy?" Past memories began to flood my mind. I was recalling times that she would go off on me for not returning her emails promptly. I thought that she was being sweet and it made me feel loved. I began to wonder if she really wanted to hear from me, or if she was wondering whether I found out about the affair yet. I thought about many overlooked details from various conversations and quickly realized that I was naïve.

I trusted them way too much, and that was my downfall. My mind continued to flash back to many of the red flags that I once ignored. I thought about the time that Aunt K tried to plant a bug in my ear. I didn't take her too seriously back then because she was a known trouble maker. In my heart, I felt it was impossible for two people that I loved so dearly to betray me.

"Hello," I answered my ringing phone quickly.

"Your best friend was over at my house last night." She began to speak without so much as a hello.

"Really?" My brow raised in confusion. "She never mentioned that she stopped by."

She chuckled with satisfaction. "Yeah, that's because she didn't want you to know what she was doing."

"Hmm, and what was she doing?" I asked, now more curious than I was originally.

"Girl she was playing your man real close. Much too close for my liking." she chuckled with enthusiasm, I could tell that she was enjoying relaying the news to me.

"So what were they doing?" I asked, already prepared not to believe her. I knew how she was. She loved drama.

"She was sitting on the edge of the chair along with him, damn near sitting on his lap and trust me there were plenty of available seats. Then she followed him around the house like a puppy. Where he went, she went. I watched her hang onto every word that came out of his mouth. It was completely inappropriate."

"They're like family" I replied reluctantly.

"Family or not, she shouldn't be behaving in the way that she was. Even when he stepped away to smoke a cigarette, she jumped up and ran behind him in the hallway. A few minutes afterwards, his friend ended up going out into the hallway to say something to him and she jumped back to create distance between them, as if they were doing something they had no business doing. It wasn't only me. Tee, everyone thought that their actions were strange." She rambled.

"No Aunt K, that's crazy. There's no way the two of them would be doing anything like that. You don't know what you're talking about." I refuted.

She laughed heartily and then began to speak again. "You can brush things off, if you like. I know what I witnessed. Homegirl wants your man. Mark my words. I am not the only one that feels that way either. Everyone was buzzing about her actions the moment that she left. You know that's how her aunt used to get down too, right?" she added looking to gossip.

"I guess it runs in the family" she continued, chuckling at her own joke.

"I don't have time to worry about that. I have to figure out what's going on with my case" I responded firmly.

"Yeah I know, but you should think long and hard before you take that time." she advised in an even firmer tone.

"Alright, I have to go." I said cutting the conversation short. I was growing increasingly tired of the negativity and I didn't want to hear it anymore.

"She's just trying to start drama, like she always does."I thought.

Back then, I tried hard to purge the conversation from my mind but was unsuccessful. I ended up telling my best friend and she immediately became irate. My accusations offended her. I ended up feeling bad that I brought it up in the first place. The two of us had our first big fight and didn't speak for many weeks following.

As I was shaken from my thoughts I began to feel stupid. It bothered me that I couldn't see it coming. It also bothered me that everyone knew of their relationship except for me. I didn't speak to anyone for a few weeks after. I closed myself off to both the free world and the prison world, needing to privately process all that was happening. Several times I attempted to pray, but my thoughts were constantly wandering off towards the two of them.

The harsh feeling of loneliness returned and It was worse than ever because I had no one to call for comfort. She was my person. The women around me often caught me staring into space. They would snap their fingers in front of my face to tell me that it was mealtime. I was living on another planet.

After much thought, I decided to reach out to her. Even though I was hurting, and I knew what the deal was, I still needed to hear her voice. I needed to hear her side of the story. We went through too much together and I couldn't write her off without allowing her to explain herself. I was willing to risk looking foolish to the world in an effort to give my best friend another chance. In my heart, she would never purposely disrespect me on this level. Our bond was too solid for that. She was the one person in the world that I could share my deepest secrets with. I was angry with my husband, but my best friend is the one that made it hurt.

THE INFAMOUS PHONE CALL

"Hey girl" she answered excitedly. I immediately recognized the phoniness in her voice. There was a nervous energy surrounding the call, that I never detected before.

"How could you?" I blurted out, I didn't want to waste any time beating around the bush. I checked my emotions before getting on the phone, but they quickly began getting the best of me. My voice cracked within the first ten seconds.

"Wait a minute, I can barely hear you." She spoke into the phone. I knew that this was simply a stall tactic.

"You can hear me." I boomed with much bass in my voice.

"Tee, I'm on the bus. I don't know what's going on." she said.

I didn't care for anything that she was saying. I instantly began cursing her out. I never experienced such a combination of emotions flowing through me. I wanted to kick her in the face hard, but I also wanted to cry on her shoulder. I wanted her to hug me and comfort me. She was the person I would confide in during situations like this. I was confused.

"No, it's not true." She lied weakly. "I would never do anything like that to you. People are spreading rumors and I don't understand why. I was hearing them too but I didn't want to tell you" she added.

I didn't believe her lies one bit. She may have been able to fool others but she could never fool me. I knew her too well and I knew that she was lying through her overlapping teeth. I was becoming increasingly angry by the second.

It was evident that she didn't respect me enough to keep it real with me. I began to scream at the top of my lungs. I was fed up with her lack of accountability. I gave the entire unit a show. Everyone present had a front row seat to my pain. I threatened her and called her everything under the sun. This bitch had the audacity to get smart with me.

"I may as well go ahead and fuck him now, since you already believe I did." She spoke up once she finally got the opportunity to chime in.

If I had the ability to break out of prison, I would have. I wanted to stomp a mud hole into her. I could not believe the nerve of this bitch to chuckle after saying something so classless. I didn't have the opportunity to say another word. Shortly after she hung up in my ear. I stared at the phone in my hand like a foreign object.

Immediately, I began calling my husband non-stop praying that he would answer. After the tenth attempt, I just slid to the floor directly underneath the phone. The women on the unit didn't bother me at all. I was grateful that they allowed me to have my moment. I sat crying silently, while everyone moved about around me. *"She got me so good."* The pain in my heart was like nothing I had ever experienced before. I couldn't fathom in my mind how two people that I loved so much could hurt me so badly. I never even saw it coming.

SWALLOWING BETRAYAL

The sting of betrayal changed me. I was broken internally and failed to process it in a healthy way. The ordeal transformed me into a grumpy and mean person that I didn't recognize. My happy-go-lucky nature was replaced by suspiciousness and skepticism. I didn't trust a soul any longer inside or outside of prison. I questioned everything. Immersed in despair, once again I began to displace my anger. Instead of fighting for healing, I was solely focused on revenge.

I can recall envisioning the two of them interacting as a couple. Daily I would do this, only to sicken myself. I couldn't stop myself from thinking about them no matter how hard I tried. My husband replaced me with the closest person to me and I couldn't believe it. I was guilt-ridden each time that I thought of my children. I left them in the care of monsters. It was evident that every decision that I made up until this point was a bad one and I was paying the cost dearly.

I was no longer comfortable with my children interacting with my ex-best friend because I didn't trust her. I didn't know what other damage she might be capable of. Many people assumed that I was being spiteful, but truthfully, I was afraid. I would cringe hearing stories of her chastising my son and I didn't want to give her any more leverage than she already had. Unfortunately, my request fell on deaf ears, as I found out that my husband was often taking my oldest son to her house along with him. I later discovered that Aunt K was complaining about caring for my baby, which is why he didn't have a choice but to bring him along. I felt violated and disrespected by his actions especially because I didn't know the reasoning behind it. As a result, the stress began to manifest on my physical being. I saw my naturally thick hair falling out in clumps.

Bit by bit, pieces of the puzzle came together, as random people fed information to me. I experienced one sting after the other as I found out that my husband was audacious enough to allow my ex-bestie to drive my car. I even heard that many times they would share my bed in our apartment.

Instead of closing myself off from the information to save my heart, I would obsessively inquire to hear more. I wasn't able to recognize that the additional details weren't beneficial to me. The information only added pain to the heartache that I was feeling. My focus should have been on healing, however I chose to add fuel to the already burning fire on the inside of me. I was caught in an unhealthy cycle of pushing to learn more of their relationship. The only thing that I wanted was to be released from prison, just so that I could beat her ass.

My self esteem plummeted as I started to believe that I wasn't worth love and loyalty. Pessimistic thoughts of my entire life would overtake me. I directed everything inward. I tied together the abandonment by my parents, so called friends and now my husband. *"It must be me. I'm not lovable. I must be cursed."*

I reasoned that I contributed to attracting all of what came to me. This led to me becoming insecure with my decision making. I didn't want to deal with those feelings so I displaced my hurt by taking it out on others that were around me. My words became aggressive and abrasive. I began indulging in gossip and bickering. I became even more submerged into my environment and I could no longer keep the negative stench off me. In fact, I reeked of it. Confrontations became a regular offense for me. My appearance also suffered as I no longer cared about how others perceived me.

With the sudden realizations, my life plummeted beyond reach. I listened to no one as I was completely content with staying in my own head. I also didn't want anything to do with the word of God and it wasn't because I was angry with him. I just didn't want to talk to him because it was obvious to me that I wasn't one of his favorites.

IS IT OVER?

The day finally arrived when I was able to reach my husband. As soon as I heard his voice on the line, the first thing to fly out my mouth was that I didn't want to reconcile our marriage. I was angry and fed up that it had taken such a long time for me to reach him. *"What if I really needed something? He really doesn't care."* It angered me that he was more concerned with avoiding the obvious subject. My mind was made up.

"Yea, yea, I know," he replied, cutting me short. He never gave me the opportunity to finish my sentence and I didn't know how to interpret that. Insecurity consumed me.

"Is he happy with her? Was he waiting for me to say that? Maybe he's happy that he doesn't have to sneak around with her anymore. Did he ever love me?" Thoughts ran through my mind like an olympic track star.

As we conversed, I noticed that he was speaking to me as if I was the one that did something wrong to him. He went on to reveal that my ex-best friend revealed things that I shared with her in confidence. He was coming down hard on me. The script was flipped.

The hurt began to bubble over as I felt as if I was betrayed twice. She used my own words against me knowing that she had to change his perception of me in an effort to win him over. I was seething as I listened to him reveal more of what he knew. In response, I chose to fight fire with fire, I began telling him all of her dirty little secrets. I allowed her foulness to alter my principles. My brokenness caused me to stoop just as low as she had.

Our conversations were unhealthy and toxic. I could tell that he was fully committed to her by the way that he defended her. It was in the same fashion that he once defended me. The narrative completely changed, instead of him explaining his indiscretions, I was finding myself on the defense.

I sensed that he was more entertained by our conversations rather than concerned about the pain that he was causing. At that point, I decided to hang up. I no longer cared to waste money, especially since he wasn't providing for me anymore.

I hadn't seen any of this coming. Involuntarily, my mind began to drift back to reminisce on how things used to be between us before I went to prison. I started having flashbacks of when my husband and I used to double date with my Bestie. I also thought about all us being together at her house for the holidays. Everyone in the neighborhood knew that we were together. When he used to hangout outside, everyone used to get mad when they saw my car pulling up because they knew that it meant that he was leaving the scene. It was no secret that he was always on my side, it didn't matter if he was arguing with his own family.

This was the same man who used to travel with me, each time that I had to travel for my case. He was by my side for every court date and doctor's appointment. He even accompanied me to church. Whatever I needed or wanted from him was available to me. I even thought about the time that he had gotten a lawsuit lump-some and handed me the debit card to the account that had all of the money.

This just didn't make any sense. Something just wasn't right. Shaken from my thoughts, I knew that I had to do something. Despite all of his shenanigans, I wanted to forgive him but he was making it extremely difficult. Deep down inside, I still wanted my family and my marriage to work. I especially wanted to work on things for the sake of my children. I just needed him to get on board.

I began to envision life after my release. I knew for certain that I didn't want to be a single mother of two boys. I had no idea what it would be like to raise two boys at all, let alone as a single woman. My oldest son would be seven and my younger son would be four at the time of my release. Raising them by myself hadn't been in my plans.

I wanted to talk things out and express myself to my husband, but his ignorance and disrespect was turning me off.

After much thought, I decided to reach out to him again. He picked up and this time I proceeded to reveal my vulnerability while sharing my thoughts and feelings. Surprisingly he agreed with me. He also wanted to be a family. At that point, I began to ask many questions. I needed to talk about what happened in an effort to forgive and heal.

As I asked, he answered. I called him several times throughout the day and he answered my call each time. It felt good to hear him apologize. He also revealed how the affair began. His story was that they indulged in taking ecstasy pills together and that's how it began initially. I guess that meant that he wasn't in his right mind.

Although this new information was quite a shock to my system, I kept an open mind as he revealed the details that I felt I needed to know. I was careful not to respond angrily or aggressively. I didn't want him shutting down the conversation. All in all, he believed that it was loneliness and depression that drove him to her. Before our last conversation ended that night, he assured me that he would break things off. He then mentioned that he would take our kids south for a while to clear his head and spend time with his sister.

We ended the call on a high note or so I thought. In the back of my mind, I understood that there was a possibility that he would retreat to her again. I still had time left to serve and I didn't want to be naïve in thinking that he would turn over a new leaf and wait for me even though that's what he said.

After speaking with him, I was able to understand the sadness and loneliness that he felt as a result of my incarceration, even though I was still furious at his lack of self-control. It had been a long time since things were pleasant between us and I wanted to keep it that way so I didn't share my negative feelings. Instead I focused on the positive. I was happy to hear him taking accountability for spending so much time with her. He understood that his choices contributed to their affair. He also emphasized that initially, she was the one that was pursuing and seducing him. Eventually he became weak. I wished he had been more mindful of his vows, but the damage was already done.

Our conversation revealed to me that my husband was not built as tough as I originally thought. He was emotionally weak, and I could hear it in his voice. My own expectations failed me as I believed that he had the utmost respect for me. He could've slept with anyone else. The reason he chose her puzzled me. The much-needed closure helped my anger to subside. Instead, embarrassment began to consume me. Despite my ill feelings, I was still determined to hold on and see how things would play out.

Unfortunately my hopes were deflated within a few weeks, as his promises didn't last long. I could no longer reach him easily, and this time I knew why. I knew in my heart that he was back with her. I received all the confirmation that I needed when I called and emailed and received no response for days at a time. It bothered me that he didn't have the balls to be honest and straightforward with me. By this time, I was away for almost three years. I saw that my absence was enough to prove the cliche saying true. "Out of sight, out of mind." No matter how hard I tried, I couldn't bear in mind how the two of them could continue an illicit relationship as if I was never coming back.

"Is this what I get in return for being his wife and bearing his first-born son?" I felt as if he was punishing me for my decision to be a stand-up person. All of his actions conveyed that he just didn't care. I began to feel the burden of stress again. My thoughts were running wild with wonder. *"Did he return from South Carolina? Did she follow him down there? How and when did they rekindle? Did he ever really try to separate?"* My thoughts were sending me right back into the destructive pattern that I had fought to free myself from.

Eventually I put on my big girl panties and waved the white flag. My marriage was over and there wasn't anything that I could do about it. I placed myself in this situation and I had to be accountable enough to bear the consequences. I had to accept things as they were. I forced myself to stop reaching out completely because I needed to preserve my mental health. Acceptance was a big pill to swallow. I began to understand that I couldn't force change on anyone except myself.

Some months passed before I received correspondence from my husband again. On one random morning, in my inbox there it was. An email from him, asking for a divorce. The email didn't contain any elaboration. It was short, simple, and insensitive. I was destroyed all over again. I knew the day would come but I didn't think that it would be so soon. I felt like I was dreaming. Suddenly I became nauseous and hot. My tearfilled eyes were now wide open. I had no choice but to swallow the demise of my marriage.

MOVING ON

As if my circumstances couldn't get any worse, I found myself with even more stress to endure. The prison administration came around on one random morning to announce that Danbury was soon to be converted into a men's institution. They went on to explain that renovations would need to be made throughout the units and that we were responsible for a large part.

Soon after, almost all jobs throughout the compound were reassigned to construction. Thankfully, I didn't have to deal with that because I was still working in the kitchen and staff and inmates would always need to eat until the end. The inmates who didn't have jobs in or outside of the compound became mandated construction workers. If they refused to work, they would be written up. Many of the women tried to get medical excuses from the infirmary, but the medical staff was hip to the games. I witnessed modern day slavery happen right before my eyes.

This news meant that we would all be transferred to an alternative prison soon. They told us that although we had to leave, they would try to keep us as close to home as possible. I now had a new stress to add to my growing list. My entire life was about to change.

I really didn't need or want change. In fact, most of the women didn't. Everything that I worked to establish behind the wall would shift. Including my money, the cost of calls and potential visits with my children. The thought of moving was traumatizing and overwhelming. It brought me back to the time I spent in foster care, where there was no stability and worry of constantly moving.

The first step of the transfer process was to become designated. FBOP would decide where we were headed. There was a good chance that I would transfer back to Brooklyn. There were pros and cons in going back to Brooklyn. This meant that I would be closer to my children but it would also mean harder time spent. In addition, my movement and my money would also be limited.

Many factors would be considered before I became designated. Those factors included bed space in my home facility, separation orders, disciplinary record, and a slew of other factors. On most occasions inmates are sent to the prison closest to their home state, however there were instances where inmates ended up randomly designated to a facility across the country. We had no say in where we were sent. This was just another reminder that we were nothing more than a number. Not knowing where I would end up, caused me an extensive amount of anxiety.

I became super depressed during the waiting period. Many women around me were experiencing depression as well. Some women spent twenty to thirty years in proximity with one another and feared being separated from their partners and friends. I sympathized deeply with the women serving life sentences. It was more than devastating to them because this was their home, and they were being uprooted.

Additionally, transferring also meant a significant loss of property. The FBOP had a strict policy regarding the amounts on items being permitted to ship. This meant that if you previously stocked up on items, such as ten bars of soap and they only permitted five in the transfer, then this would mean that the remaining five would have to be given away or trashed. Transferring was a big headache overall.

Many of us became attached and possessive over commissary. We didn't realize it was cheap stuff that really didn't matter. Thinking back on it makes me sad. I can recall times when inmates would physically fight over ramen noodles and processed chicken pouches. I too became obsessed with collecting commissary. I wanted to keep as much as possible. I developed a fear of running out of food and hygiene products. Even though I was always hustling, I never told anyone in the free world. I always pretended that I didn't have anything whenever my friends or loved ones asked. This practice was typical amongst all of us. It wasn't because we were trying to get over, it was simply to ensure that we always had.

A DEAL GONE BAD

Prior to my incarceration, I had a serious problem with controlling my emotions and maintaining self-control. That issue grew and amplified a thousand times after living in a prison environment. In prison, having tantrums was acceptable and considered to be the norm. During the times when I was experiencing high stress, I often found trouble. I didn't have a healthy way of expressing myself. With daunting thoughts of my appending transfer and complete lack of support, I moved deeper into survival mode.

I began to take more risk as I became obsessed with stacking as much money as I could before the prison closed. Every single day people were being called to pack up and I began to get nervous. I knew how to work in Danbury, but I wasn't so sure that I was going to be able to work the same way in a new environment. Many of the women who served time at other institutions prior warned that there was nowhere like Danbury. Danbury FCI could be described as laxed.

I came up with the bright idea to make hooch and sell it. For those of you that are unfamiliar, hooch is basically homemade liquor, made predominantly out of citrus fruits. I sampled some, but I had never made it on my own. Hooch tasted just as potent as real liquor. It was considered to be an expensive commodity in prison, and I had access to the ingredients. I knew that I could potentially make a lot of money. My only reservation was getting caught, due to the consequences that it carried. Not only would I lose several good days, but I would also lose all privileges such as phone calls, commissary, and email. This was considered to be one of the most serious infractions of all.

Although I knew that it was a serious risk, I needed the money. I was already running low on funds so a few hundred dollars would hold me over for the next few months. This would allow me to transfer comfortably and allow me time to plan my next course of action. Plus I already had a lineup of willing customers. I just needed to start getting the ingredients together. I connected with a stud who was assigned to the same unit as I was. I'll call her Bree. Bree and I decided to partner after I proposed my idea to her. She would also teach me how to make hooch.

My plan was to steal all of the ingredients then have them passed off to Bree, similar to how I passed off the vegetables. Bree would handle the responsibility of making the hooch, hiding it as well as the processing. I agreed to give her half of the proceeds. Once the agreement was made, I began sending the ingredients her way through other inmates. As our concoction was brewing, she and I became cool with one another. We began talking more frequently. Unfortunately for the both of us, our budding friendship didn't last long. The two of us ended up in a petty argument.

A few days passed and the two of us were still not speaking to one another but I didn't think our lack of communication would affect our business. I was still working to secure one more item, as the two of us agreed to allow the drink to sit longer in order to gain potency.

One morning Bree's bunkie came to work smelling of alcohol. I inquired whether she was drinking or not. I was already aware that if she were drinking, it was most certainly my product. She confirmed my thoughts. Bree was in fact selling our product. I was furious and I planned to confront her as soon as they opened the kitchen doors and allowed us to exit for laundry runs.

When the doors opened, I rushed to the unit. I went straight to the spot where the hooch was hidden, only to find that it was no longer there. This frustrated me even more. Instantly, I went looking for Bree. My time was limited, and I would soon be due back at work. Not long after, I spotted her strolling across the compound with her girlfriend as if she didn't have a care in the world. I broke into a light sprint in an effort to catch up to them.

"What's up with the stuff, is it done?" I asked rhetorically, since I was fully aware of what she had done.

"What stuff?" she smirked. It was then that it dawned on me that she had given her bunkie the hooch on purpose. She wanted me to find out. She knew that we worked together. This woman was provoking me for no reason, all because of a small argument.

"You think I'm just going to allow you to do this? How do you think I'm going to take this?" I replied. She laughed heartily as if I was a big joke.

"Take it however you like, Girl. Remember I had to get the last item myself that you never sent. " She said before walking off in the opposite direction.

Something overtook me, as I decided right then and there to beat her ass. I was tired of being disrespected. Bree wasn't a small girl, but I also wasn't intimidated by her size. I didn't want to go back to the SHU, so I knew I had to be smart about the way I attacked her. I wanted to be smart about my moves this time around so I walked to my cell to secure my belongings first. I couldn't afford to lose my property in the instance that I went to the SHU. Next, I ran to find my homegirl who I knew didn't have any reservations when it came to fighting. I'll call her kim. When I found Kim, she was sleeping peacefully. She was upset that I had awakened her, but quickly shook it off.

"Come with me and make sure I'm good," I said. She was one of those friends that was always ready for drama.

"Where is she?" she asked while getting dressed quickly.

Kim didn't need many details to be all in. The moment that she was finished dressing, we were on our way to the woman's cell. It was about to go down. As we got closer, I thought about Bree being three times my size, and sudden nervousness was setting in.

"You better not let her get the best of me." I told my friend.

My palms were sweating, and I could hear my heart beating outside my chest. When I got to the door, her bunkie immediately moved out of the way. She must've sensed what was about to go down. I saw that she was still drinking her hooch and that gave me the fuel that I needed.

When she and I locked eyes, all nervousness dissipated. I ran into her cell and cracked her in the face with my plastic commissary mug. I struck her with blow after blow until the mug broke. After the mug broke, I dropped it then continued striking her with a closed fist. As if the blows weren't enough, I dragged her outside of the cell by her dreads.

It was at that moment, I messed up. Everyone on the lower level had a bird's eye view of what was happening. A small crowd began to gather around us quickly. I didn't care about getting caught anymore. I was in a zone. There was much anger built up on the inside of me. Unbeknownst to her, she wasn't only getting it for what she had done. She was also getting it for what my husband was doing.

After a few more moments, my friend pulled me away. She was yelling that I had done enough. At that point, I released my grip and began to walk away, but not before looking back at Bree. It felt good to observe her scrambling around on the floor looking for her glasses. *"I bet the next person will think twice before disrespecting me"* I thought.

"That's how we do it in New York." A random woman yelled as she bent down beside Bree who was still down.

I turned my focus forward and proceeded to walk out of the unit smoothly. It felt good to be able to stand up for myself. I handled the disrespect and still made it back to work as if nothing ever happened. I didn't tell a soul what I had done.

THE AFTERMATH

The day went by smoothly and I completed my work duties quickly. Towards the end of the day, I forgot about the fight altogether. All was well in my eyes. Neither of us landed in the SHU and I was able to release some steam. Unfortunately, that solace came to a halt as soon as the dining room opened for lunch. I had a rude awakening. There was chatter everywhere. The word around town was that Bree was angry and looking for revenge.

She told just about everyone that she was planning to cut my face as soon as she got a chance. She even stretched the truth by telling everyone that I had snuck her. I wasn't bothered by that part because I knew what really happened. She saw me coming, straight on. Nevertheless, I couldn't believe that she was planning to cut me over a fist fight, when she was the one who initiated the disrespect. I got scared, but I didn't want to show it. I wasn't ready for things to escalate to this level. I guessed the old saying, you win some and you lose some went out the window in prison.

I now had an even bigger problem on my hands than I had before. I had already lost out on profits from the hooch, now I needed to watch my back. I was beginning to realize that none of this was worth the headache. As it was nearing time for me to get off, I looked up and saw Kim walking towards me. She would often pick me up from work then we would chill together, talk and play games. So it wasn't odd to see her.

However this time was different. The look she wore on her face was serious. I noticed right away that she kept her hands tucked in the pockets of her fleece sweater. When I approached her, she immediately relayed the same news that everyone else told me. Then, she handed me a combination lock tucked in a sock. Next, she instructed me to keep my hands wrapped around the sock and keep a firm grip on it.

She then revealed that she also had a lock in a sock. Together the two of us began to walk through the compound. I felt as if people were looking at me differently, it seemed like they didn't want to get too close to me. I could have been paranoid, but I really felt like everyone knew that this girl was planning to cut me.

"I'm not going to lie, friend, I'm sort of nervous." I confided in Kim.

"Girl nervous for what? I'm not going to allow her to get close to you. We're going to beat her to a pulp." She said without any hesitation.

"Omg, beat her to a pulp? What have I gotten myself into?" I thought.

For two days I couldn't sleep properly. I slept with one eye open. Kim and I took shifts. When I slept, she stood watch and vice versa. Nightly I had recurring nightmares of Bree cutting me along the side of my face. When I took showers, Kim would sit by the door of the shower with a lock in a sock, reading magazines until I was finished. The feeling of paranoia was a horrible one that I wouldn't wish on my worst enemy. I was beginning to regret everything that I had done. My saving grace was on one evening when the officers secured the compound stopping all movement.

"Vulcain please report to the lieutenants office immediately" They called me to the lieutenants office in an effort to inspect me for bruises. Someone had written a cop out and snitched on us. It was obvious that the two of us were guilty as charged and we were both cuffed and marched across the compound to the SHU, one after another. I never thought that I could experience joy going to solitary confinement. Oh how happy I was to know that I no longer had to watch my back.

When I arrived at the SHU, I was searched, stripped and issued that infamous orange jumpsuit again. As soon as they locked me into a cell, I was knocked out cold. I slept for two days straight without a care in the world. No nightmares. No worries. I slept until I couldn't sleep anymore. I remember getting up and just staring at the rusted bars in front of me. I hadn't prayed in such a long time and I wasn't sure if God could still hear me. I was beginning to see that my way of doing things wasn't working. *"God, there has to be a better way, please just get me out of here."* I thought.

TRANSFERRING OUT

I never made it out of the SHU that time. The prison administration released Bree from the SHU after she served her time. I on the other hand was held until it was time for me to transfer out of Danbury. This was somewhat relieving to me because I didn't have access to a phone or a computer. The absence of both surprisingly brought relief. Without a phone or a computer, It would be impossible to inquire about my husband and his new woman and the bonus was that I didn't have to worry about Bree anymore.

I wasn't clear as to why the prison administration ordered a separation order, but I was aware of what it meant. We couldn't serve time in the same prison ever again, and if we happened to land in the same facility then one of us would always be sent to the SHU. It was a little annoying being placed in the SHU for an extended amount of time, however it wasn't my first rodeo so I was accustomed to it.

The part that bothered me most, was missing out on the opportunity to collect the money that was owed to me on the compound. The other thing that bothered me was wearing that same awful orange jumpsuit for days. That was something that I could never get used to.

There was a bit of gossip in the SHU. Apparently the other women were spreading rumors. Bree told everyone around the prison that I requested the separation order because I was afraid of her. Of course, that wasn't the case, but I was okay with letting the people think whatever they wanted. My face wasn't cut and that was enough satisfaction for me. I was going through enough and I wasn't interested in thinking about a narrative that I couldn't control.

I noticed a change with the officers. The ones that worked the SHU were becoming increasingly aggressive and disrespectful. Even though I wasn't directly affected, it bothered me. I reasoned that they felt empowered to get away with things that they normally wouldn't do because the prison was closing soon. I watched officers remove the mattress from a woman's cell forcing her to sleep on a hard sheet of metal. She hadn't done anything to deserve that. They did this to her out of sheer retaliation.

I was amongst the last women to be designated to a prison. I remained in solitary confinement for almost seven months. Thankfully my time locked in was better spent this time around as I began being intentional about getting myself together.

This time, I utilized the time to pray, read and reflect on everything that happened in my life up until that point. I reflected a lot on my past mistakes and realized that somewhere along the line I lost focus. My goal was to do my time and get home to my children, instead I was allowing my time to do me. Prison drama cost me months of good time that I could've spent with my kids. It was in those moments of reflection that I realized that there wasn't anything I had done that was worth time spent away from my children.

I found out that I was designated to Philadelphia Federal Detention Center. Philly wasn't Brooklyn so I was a little bummed. I really wanted to be in my own city but I was grateful that I hadn't been sent to Florida or somewhere farther. I was hopeful that when I got my visiting privileges back, I could possibly receive a visit from my children since it wasn't too far. I was long overdue and being locked away in SHU hadn't afforded me the opportunity to speak with them as often as I would have liked. I didn't like how my life was playing out and I made a decision right then and there to change. I was betting on my renewed positive mindset to help me navigate differently.

In the midst of that, my friend Kim happened to come to SHU. I joked that she missed me. She had gotten into some trouble of her own while I was locked away and ended up in a fight of her own. The officers knew how tight we were, so they allowed us to bunk together.

Having her company made the days go by much faster. We told one another stories until the wee hours of the morning. I also wasn't so shy using the bathroom in front of a friend, which was a bonus.

We were extremely happy on the day that we were transferred as we were the very last group to leave the facility. We were informed that we would be temporarily placed at MDC Brooklyn and then transported to our designated facilities a few days afterward. I personally didn't care where I was going, I was just tired of being in solitary confinement. I wanted to see the sunlight badly. My skin was so pale that it appeared almost ghost white. It also didn't help that we didn't have the luxury of lotion.

New York City is a place that never stops growing and evolving. I never realized how fast paced my city was until I was removed from it. I felt like a tourist as I rode through the city on the way to MDC Brooklyn. Everything and everyone looked much different from what I last encountered. Things like green cab cars and different license plate designs stuck out to me. It hadn't been that long since I was gone, yet everything changed so drastically. It felt weird to see that the world was moving on without me. I felt as if I was frozen in time.

When we finally arrived at Brooklyn MDC, it was soothing to hear HOT 97 blasting through a nearby radio. My friend began dancing to a song in the holding cell. The vibe all around us was just different. She was excited about being in New York, and I was happy to finally be out of the SHU. Unfortunately, that happiness didn't last too long. We were later searched, then issued orange jumpers instead of tan uniforms.

Of course, orange jumpers meant that we were going back to the SHU. We tried to explain to the officers that we were finished with our time in the SHU, but our pleas fell on deaf ears. They told us that they had to sort out our paperwork and when they did, they would let us out. Our paperwork never did get sorted out. I believed that we were deemed problematic and left in the SHU because we weren't assigned to that facility. We were still in the midst of transferring and we weren't their problem.

There was a huge difference between Danbury's SHU and MDC Brooklyn's SHU. Danbury's SHU was a luxury to say the least. Danbury's SHU had bars that we could yell between and talk to one another, we would also pass magazines and other items. However, in MDC Brooklyn, The SHU was a steel box that was soundproof. We were closed off from the world. Thankfully they allowed the two of us to bunk together, otherwise I probably would've lost my mind.

There was no sound, outside of when the officers came to bring us food or to handcuff us to take us to the showers. To make matters worse, Kim and I started bickering back and forth about every little thing. The mounting pressure of the situation was beginning to weigh on us both causing us to become argumentative and grumpy. Our relationship became awkward. As a result we began speaking to one another far less than we had before.

In Brooklyn MDC SHU, it took a long time to receive a commissary sheet to order personal items. We had to use state soap which was extremely harsh on the skin. I had become accustomed to Danbury allowing us to shop at the commissary weekly for hygiene items. Here, three weeks passed before we were allowed to purchase toiletries. This new SHU was extremely uncomfortable for me. I was skinny, ashy, pale and depressed. Not to mention my hair was severely breaking off again.

Many of those nights, I cried beneath my blanket, replaying everything that I had experienced over and over in my mind, much like a broken tape. My regrets were piled up high. Sadly, the highlight of my day was when I was asleep. During my waking hours, I felt like I was being tortured in hell.

After about a month, they released me. It was time to complete my journey to Philadelphia. It was bittersweet to leave Kim behind as we had grown so close in Danbury. Me leaving meant that she would be all alone and I felt bad for her. Even though we hadn't been getting along so well, I still would miss her. When the time came for me to depart, the two of us hugged and I was cuffed and sent on my way. A new journey for me was about to begin once again.

OKLAHOMA TRANSFER CENTER

Traveling was always tiring and draining, The process took up the entire day. There were several long waiting periods, one of which was spent in various holding cells with several other women and a toilet. I drank very little and trained myself to hold my pee. Nobody was about to see my behind tooted up in the air. I would always maintain some level of pride.

Ninety nine percent of the time, we all had to go through the Federal transfer center when moving. It was located in Oklahoma. I was annoyed that even though my trip was technically from Connecticut to Philadelphia, I still had to go through the transfer center.

The most interesting part was seeing the guys who were also traveling between prisons, on the plane to the facility. The women who were transferring opted for the tightest jumpers and would find a way to conceal a little vaseline in order to keep their lips shining. Some women would even switch their hips as we left the van and boarded the plane. They were being sexy with shackles on and trying to get peeks at the guys while we were in the air. For the entire flight, the U.S. marshals would constantly tell them to turn their heads frontwards. I thought it was so funny. I wasn't the least bit interested. *"What can a man in jail do for me?"* I thought to myself.

I also knew that I looked crazy. After spending several months in the SHU, I was pale, and my hair was dry and nappy. I had large, unkempt braids that I did myself in an effort to prevent my hair from breaking off. I couldn't wait to get to the transfer center so that I could finally take a long hot shower and properly groom myself. I knew someone there would know how to braid. I was hoping to get my hair done and feel like a person again. In the SHU, I hadn't seen a mirror, but I had a good idea of how I looked and it was uncomfortable being around all of these people while looking so bad. I knew that I resembled a cave woman.

Oklahoma was okay. I was happy to be back in population and mingling amongst other people. My standards of prison life weren't so high anymore. I was able to shower every single day, multiple times if I chose to and for that I was immensely grateful. The meals weren't too bad either. I met other women who knew of some of the women that I was incarcerated with at Danbury. Together we all told a bunch of stories and gossiped until there was nothing else to talk about. I read a lot as well. They had some good books to read in the library and when I didn't want to read any longer, I had the option of watching television. Prayer also took up much of my time.

I was relieved to finally get my hair done again, for me that was one of the best parts. I finally felt decent as I humbly and patiently waited to be transferred. I was enjoying the usage of my three-hundred phone minutes as well. I hadn't been able to jones on the phone like that in months, and I was enjoying it. My minutes would reset again once I reached Philly, so I utilized the extra time to catch up with my children and friends. I put my pride and ego to the side and begged a few of my friends for some money to hold me over as well.

In hindsight I realized that it was sad that it took many harsh and unpleasant experiences for me to become grateful. Although I had lost so much I was appreciative that things hadn't turned out much worse. I remained in Oklahoma for a few days, before moving again. Once I said my goodbyes to my new homegirls, I prepared myself mentally for another long day of travel.

As I sat waiting to get cuffed and shackled in the holding cell, I realized that a tremendous amount of time lapsed. Many of the other women around me agreed that it was taking a long time to board the plane. After inquiring with the marshalls, we learned that it was because Chris Brown was amongst the men boarding the plane with us. There was additional protocol in place, along with tons of additional Marshalls traveling with us.

"Great so now Chris Brown is slowing down the process?" I was slightly annoyed. I didn't enjoy sitting in the bullpen waiting. That part of the process was annoying. Others felt indifferent. There was a woman waiting in the same cell who was so intrigued by the fact that Chris was traveling with us.

"Quit complaining, I love that I'm waiting for Chris Brown to board the same plane that I'm boarding. Chris can put a beating on me anytime he wants to. I'm no Rihanna." One of the women spoke up in her strong country twang.

We all began to laugh. Her comment lifted the mood in the cell. Not long after we were all shackled and moved to an area reserved for boarding the plane. It was a slow walk, as we all were shackled. I was walking directly behind Chris Brown when I suddenly realized how tall and fine he was. I've never been big on the music industry, so prior to that I didn't pay much attention to him but at that moment I literally had no choice.

It had been a long time since I had seen a man that fine. I scanned his body up and down several times. There was a dope, yet unfinished tattoo on his arm. I was crushing on him hard. I couldn't help but to keep my eyes on him as we boarded the plane. The Marshalls were going extra hard warning us not to turn around once we were seated. The women were allowed to talk to one another, but not to the men at all. That didn't stop the men from calling at us.

"Yo light skin with the braids turn around." One of the guys called out to me. I kept my attention focused forward. I was too afraid to turn around. "I bet if it was Chris calling you, you'd turn around." He added, causing the entire plane to burst into laughter. I couldn't help but laugh too.

Chris was down to earth. The guys asked him a bunch of random questions and he answered real cool. He spoke about working behind the scenes of movies that he was in, and even cracked a few jokes. He was full of personality and super humble. I realized that he was a distraction that I didn't know I needed. I had a terrible fear of being on a plane handcuffed and shackled. My thoughts would go ballistic about what could happen in case of an emergency. The light-heartedness he brought helped me to forget all about that. Later on when I got the opportunity, I made sure to download a ton of his music on my MP3 player. I guess it's safe to say that I'm now a fan.

PHILADELPHIA FDC

Philly was a whole new ballgame. It was nothing like the places that I had previously been jailed in. In Philly we were locked in our cells at night as well as during count. I wasn't accustomed to that. Initially, I thought that it would be like being in the SHU. I wasn't looking forward to being locked in with anyone. I experienced enough of that. We also didn't have access to going outside, which meant no fresh air, similar to how MDC Brooklyn was set up. There was only a steel and concrete room that had steel gates throughout. Only a small amount of fresh breeze could pass though. They referred to this room as the rec deck.

Another strange thing that I found at Philly FDC was toilet bowl talking. Bowl talking was a technique developed by inmates that allowed the women to communicate with the men. They would stick their hand in the hole of the toilet and push the water backwards. After a few minutes there wouldn't be any water left in the toilet. This would allow the men and women to speak to one another. Some would even make paper mics so they didn't have to place their faces close to the toilet bowl. Bowl talking was big and many would utilize it in order to have phone sex. Sometimes the men would even arrange money to be put on the women's accounts. There were consequences for bowl talking as well. If one was caught, they would receive an infraction and continued fraternizing would result in their room being moved.

I was doing my best to avoid all drama and steer clear of the dreaded orange jumpsuit. I constantly witnessed fights and arguments breaking out all around me due to toilet bowl talking and could easily see how it added to the toxicity on the unit. I didn't want any parts of the drama, plus I also thought it was nasty. Not wanting to revert or create any new bad habits, I stayed clear of it altogether. I vowed that I would never talk in the toilet bowl because it just wasn't worth it.

It was around this time that I began to shift my perspective. When I would find myself in arguments, I would pull myself back, to avoid fights. I began to recognize that the majority of arguments were over things that were frivolous. I was finally growing and thanking God for it. As a result of my pursuit of peace and serenity, I became aligned with like minded people. Some I am grateful to still be connected to today. I had finally found a circle of people who were drama free. Together we would sit at the same table daily, telling stories, laughing, crying and making sure one another was okay. A few of us were even into knitting and crocheting like little old ladies.

I met some genuine women there and I consider it to be a blessing to have found sisterhood in a chaotic place. We were all positive. We worked our prison jobs and minded our own business. Other girls would try to hang with us, but we were locked in, so they eventually fell off. I stopped hustling as well. I just wasn't interested anymore.

One woman that was especially special to me was my bunkie. I'll call her Rain. Rain was a chubby hispanic woman who was absolutely gorgeous. She and I became good friends and that eventually turned into us having an attraction for one another. I believe that it came from spending a significant amount of time together as a result of being locked in.

It took some time but eventually we were able to discuss how we were feeling. We both decided that we shouldn't go down that road. She was afraid to act on those feelings and so was I. I shared with her my horrible experience prior and that I was extremely vulnerable as a result of what my husband was doing on the outside. I was wise enough to know that she couldn't fill my void.

One day without warning Rain kissed me, and without thinking, I kissed her back. The companionship felt good and so I didn't stop it. Even though that happened, we never went all the way as we honored the friendship much more. For me, I knew that homosexuality went against christianity and although I was tempted, I tried my best not to go down that path again. In addition, we knew that it was risky and not worth the trouble. We kept our mouths shut about it, knowing that if someone found out then they would split us up. We both didn't want to get used to someone new all over again. Overall the friendship was a positive one. We pushed one another, supported one another and were emotionally available for each other. Rain and I's friendship contained a level of intimacy that I never before experienced.

Like all prisons, it was mandatory to work, so I took a job in maintenance and was paid forty bucks a month. Daily we would go around from unit to unit, fixing stuff throughout the building. I stuck with it even when it got hard and pinched the money I had and made it work. I was changing for the better and beginning to feel good about myself again. In addition, I decided to become intentional about how I was spending my time. This was a game changer for me even though I was in a controlled environment.

Crocheting and knitting were therapeutic for me and as a result of me doing it so well, many of the women inquired about learning from me. Initially I obliged their request, but then it quickly became overwhelming. I thought that it would be easier to teach a class on it so I asked the case manager for permission. Without any reservations, she agreed. The recreational department then supplied the yarn and hooks and I got started. Many of the women signed up and I taught the class weekly. I was compensated in yarn and was okay with that because I enjoyed crocheting. It was also a plus that I had access to many colors in yarn that weren't sold through the commissary. Women would offer to buy the yarn from me, but I gave it away instead. I was aware of how carried away I could get with selling things.

I recommitted to praying more also. I was continuously asking God to forgive me every time I thought about killing my best friend.

The anger that I felt towards her was indescribable. I would often zone out and imagine myself running her over with a car. The moment I snapped back to reality, I would pray about it, but God was taking his time with me. I wasn't healing as quickly as I would have liked to. Vengeance was consuming me. Everyone I spoke to in the prison and beyond knew how trifling my best friend was. I made sure that it was no secret.

Learning about the affair disturbed much of my inner peace. I learned through this experience that spiritual warfare is a real thing. I could feel that I was engaged in battle because I was conflicted between good and evil. I consumed myself with so much of what was done to me to the point that I was filled with hatred. Unfortunately it took a long time for me to recognize that all of it had some connection to my own choices.

Aside from battling my own demons, everything was going pretty well in Philly. Up until the point where a new girl was transferred in from a prison in the south. That's when everything changed. I'll call her Sammy. Sammy was a tall, cute black girl with a southern twang. Homegirl was always wearing super tight clothes and always had makeup on her face. Her hair always stayed tight too. She reminded me of the prison fly girls that I used to hang out with at Danbury. I noticed early on that she was very messy. Sammy was also very gay.

That might not seem like it was serious enough to emphasize but in prison that was a horrible combination. Before I knew it, she began hanging around our crew. Initially, I thought it was okay because she was funny and had stories for days. She had come from a wild prison, so she used to tell us about all the fights that she and her girlfriends used to have. Through conversation, I found out that she knew some of the girls that I met back when I was in the Oklahoma transfer center.

Everything about her was entertaining, so I began to hang out with her more against my better judgment. We were all just trying to kill time, so I didn't see too much harm in listening to her talk. In comparison to other prisons, Philly was relatively calm, so we all appreciated a good laugh. Unfortunately, I ended up being a little too friendly with her. I still hadn't learned my lesson. Somehow our girl talk turned into her crushing on me.

Sammy was so cool that I totally forgot that she was a lesbian. I don't mean one of those women who were only pretending to be a lesbian in order to pass time or gay for stay as many others would say. No, she was really about that life. In the beginning I laughed it off and still maintained a level of cool with her but then she became aggressive and persistent. She had this crazy look in her eyes that told me she was dead serious. I tried to let her down gently by telling her that I wasn't gay but she wouldn't take no for an answer.

"That other girl in Danbury didn't do it right," she said boldly one day.

"Girl I don't know what you're talking about" I replied chuckling. I wasn't surprised that she knew because that's how news often traveled.

"yeah whatever" she replied slyly before walking away.

Everyone around us thought that her antics were funny but I didn't, so I started to distance myself from her. She didn't seem to get the hint because she continued to force her way into my presence. I could see that she was beginning to show signs of possessiveness. My focus was simply to stay focused. I couldn't afford to lose any more of my good time. I felt that she was trouble and I knew first hand that being gay in prison often times landed one in the SHU as it once did me.

Every night after most of us were locked in, a few inmates would volunteer to stay out to clean the housing unit. Sammy was one of them. When she was finished cleaning, she would often come to the top tier and peep into my cell window. She would wave goodnight and blow a kiss before returning to her cell for the evening.

One night, I totally forgot about Sammy and I jumped into Rain's bed playfully once we were locked in. On this particular day, Rain had an attitude with me about something silly and I was attempting to cheer her up. I tickled her then kissed her right smack on the lips. She laughed heartily at my audacity. Once I got up, she started to talk to me but then stopped. I looked up at her then she pointed towards the door which prompted me to look over to see what she was pointing to.

I saw Sammy peering in at us and I froze. My face was flushed. I wasn't too sure about how much she saw but I noticed that she didn't wave to me like she usually would. This time she was just staring at me in a trance-like manner. It felt a little creepy, but I brushed it off. I yelled goodnight to her, but she walked away without responding to me.

The next day, Sammy appeared to be withdrawn and sad. We never saw her like that before. She usually had such a strong presence in the unit. Everyone was trying to figure out what was wrong with her, but she remained in her cell for most of the day and didn't talk to anyone. I was genuinely concerned about her, so I went to her cell to ask if she was okay. She started crying hysterically and saying that it was something that she was going through at home and that she didn't feel comfortable discussing it with me. I didn't believe her.

I felt in my spirit that her sadness had something to do with me, but it wasn't confirmed. I was acquainted with her enough to realize that mentally she wasn't stable. I was accustomed to dealing with people that were off so I knew the signs. After some thought, I decided that I shouldn't push her to talk anymore for fear of her snapping. I took one last look at her, as she sat shaking and crying. I reminded her that I was available if she needed to talk and then I left her in privacy.

The following day she snapped out of her sadness and instead became angry and obnoxious. I was awakened by her voice booming from the common area. She was carrying on and cursing wildly.

117

Sammy was ranting to whoever would listen. I didn't inquire about who she was mad at because I was no longer concerned. I could see that she was looking for attention.

When she saw me, she became even more theatrical. I purposely ignored her because I felt the entire act was unnecessary. I went on to do my normal routine, which included reading, knitting, and exercising. Unfortunately, she wasn't willing to accept my ignoring her easily.

I hoped by ignoring her, there wouldn't be any confrontation, however in prison things worked very differently. Ignoring a person only seemed to drive them to further extremes. I think that she interpreted my lack of response as weakness. As time elapsed, she became more direct. I started to see that there wasn't going to be an easy way out of this. Sammy walked around for days wearing steel toe boots and her hair tied up, as if she was seeking a fight.

She was literally taunting me and if this were some months prior, I may have fallen for her trap. However, I was at the end of my sentence and the taste of freedom was on my tongue. I was more than determined not to allow anyone to tarnish that taste. I began to wish that I had never associated myself with her. It was painstakingly obvious that she was crazy.

I found myself in a conundrum. I finally found the ability to exercise self-control but was still being taunted. Unfortunately the way things worked was that my consequences would be the same consequences as hers, even if she assaulted me first and I hit back. This is why I really didn't want to fight her, but I also knew that I needed to be prepared.

Unfortunately, I couldn't be ready enough. Sammy caught me slippin when I least expected it. One afternoon after the 4 p.m. count cleared, I was cooking for our crew as usual. I was prepping everything for the microwave while locked inside of my cell. As a result of being so engulfed in preparing our meal, I didn't notice that my cell door popped open.

Suddenly, everything went black, as something hit me in my head. It only took a second for me to register what was happening, as I immediately started fighting back. I only had socks on at the time. That combined with the freshly waxed floors made it extremely difficult for me to keep my balance. Thankfully, Rain was present to separate us as she helped to free my hair from Sammy's grasp.

My focus was keeping my balance and not hitting the floor. I didn't want to be stomped in the face by those steel toe boots. I was shocked that she had come to fight me as I was beginning to think that she was all talk. Sammy was a complete psycho. *"All because of jealousy?"* I thought. Something came over her when she saw me with Rain and instead of being honest, she lied and said that she was tired of me running my mouth. I regretted being kind to her.

When the fight ended, I was furious. I had to put on makeup right away. My face was scratched and bruised. I didn't want to go to the SHU and lose any more good time, yet I also was angry about her violating me. My pride was on the line. I feared that if I let this instance go, it would only be a matter of time before the next person tried me. I wanted peace but drama found me.

After some thought, I decided that I couldn't just eat that incident. I was going to catch her slipping just like she caught me. I would try my best not to get caught by the officers or allow any of the inmates to see. Many of the inmates loved to snitch by writing cop outs. In my heart I was saddened because I really didn't want any trouble, but I just couldn't let the violation slide.

I planned to catch her coming out of the shower. I disclosed my plan to Rain and she agreed to watch my back. After waiting a full day, I decided to strike. Late in the evening after she took her shower, I turned off my cell lights and peeped through the window waiting for her to pass. As I watched her walk, I could feel my hands getting sweaty.

After a few minutes of waiting, I saw her leaving the shower and walking towards her cell. At that point, I departed from my cell nonchalantly and walked towards hers. When I got there, I saw that she was completely naked and putting lotion on her body, as if she didn't have a care in the world.

Filled with anger, I ran into her cell and pounced on her. I fought her for all of thirty seconds until I heard the officer's keys jingling. It's possible that the jingling may have been in my head because I was afraid to get caught. At that point, I ran back to my cell, upset that I didn't have an opportunity to do her in the way that she deserved but I knew that it wasn't worth getting caught.

I should've continued kicking her behind since not long after someone snitched on us. Much like clockwork they came around checking for bruises and of course my face gave it away. Even through the makeup, they could see it. The two of us were cuffed and taken to the SHU. *"I should've beat her bloody."* I thought as I sat in the SHU furious. I couldn't believe that I was working to change my life and I still ended up in an orange jumpsuit. I made the mistake of befriending a stranger too quickly.

The SHU in Philly wasn't as bad as the previous SHU that I occupied and I was grateful. I also was fortunate enough to share my cell with someone whom I knew from the unit. This allowed time to pass quickly. The woman was in SHU for a few months before my arrival, so she looked a little crazy. I ended up braiding her hair nicely. It helped time pass for me and she was beyond grateful.

Even though I was upset that I was back in orange, I promised myself that it would be my very last time. I maintained my mindset shift by reading, journaling and praying often. I didn't allow my setback to deter me from being positive. I wasn't sad this time around because I became comfortable with solitude. I decided that I wouldn't allow isolation to bother me, instead I used the opportunity to grow.

The funniest thing about my time spent in Philly's SHU, is that I ended up contradicting my former stance. I often laugh as I look back on it. Upon arrival to Philly, I judged the woman for talking to the men through the toilet bowl. After my bunkie was released, I became bored and I found myself with a toilet bowl hunny. I even figured out how to make the paper mic so that my face wouldn't be near the toilet. I got used to it like everything else. It wasn't like I had a man at home anymore. The irony in it all, taught me to never say never.

THE TRUTH IS

I never thought that I would ever talk to a man on the toilet bowl but I ended up doing it. I also never thought that I would have a sexual experience with another woman yet I found myself experimenting. Prison taught me many things about myself but one thing that was pivotal was recognizing that I often disregarded my own convictions. Many of the things that I vowed not to do, I did, which ultimately caused me to lose trust in myself.

Initially, I walked through the door judging. I was turning my nose up at others and thinking that I was better but the truth is that I wasn't. If prison didn't do anything else, it certainly humbled me. As days passed in the SHU, I began to take ownership of what I did to contribute to my atrocities. After analyzing my own receipts, I became painfully aware that I was the greatest contributor.

I chose to become grateful moving forward. Although I was at a low point in my life, I forced myself to think about what I could be thankful for. Aunt K was one person that came to mind. I couldn't help but acknowledge that even with her crafty ways, she was the one that took care of my baby. Many of the women lost their children to the system yet I never had that problem. After my reflection, I still couldn't stand Aunt K because of her controlling and manipulative ways but I couldn't help but appreciate her role in my baby's life. She took control of my child against my wishes but I realize now that through her, God was ensuring that all things were working for my good.

In addition, Aunt K agreed to allow me to move into her home once released. She didn't want me to take my baby son and I equally didn't want to rip him from her life. My husband managed to keep up with my apartment so I did have a place to stay but still I opted to be with my children. Although I didn't care for her, I thought it was quite honorable of her to be able to compromise on that level. I wouldn't have much space and would be sleeping on a bunk bed but it was well worth living in the same room as my children. I know now that God worked this out for me long before I thought of it.

As I sat in the SHU, my life began to flash before me like scenes in a movie. I thought about my faults, my weaknesses and my greed. I began to reflect on many of the poor decisions that I made, before prison and while in prison. As I sat in silence, I could hear the officers' radios going off as they passed my cell door. The sound of the radio triggered something within me. It brought me back to the sound of the police radios from the day that I got arrested. I then flashed back to one of the most traumatic days of my life.

4 ½ years prior

It was that time of the month and I was grumpy. I didn't feel like swiping that day but I pushed myself out of pure greed. Aunt K was babysitting my son and repeatedly called to ask me when I was planning to come back. I was far away but I didn't want to tell her that. In an effort to deflect, I asked her "What do you want me to pick up for you? I'll get anything you want."

She wanted household items such as sheet sets and laundry detergent. In an effort to pacify her, I did something that I normally never do. I got off of the line that I was already in, to backtrack and shop for the items that she requested.

While I was shopping, I saw my best friend and her aunt also proceed to do the same. We were distracted and we weren't paying attention like we normally would. Consequently, we ended up staying inside of the store much longer than normal. We were too comfortable and being sloppy, having no idea that this was getting ready to cost us dearly.

Finally we all made our way to the cash register. The cards this time around seemed to have relatively low limits. As a result, I needed to initiate several small transactions. That took extra time as well. I had a stack of credit cards and I was swiping one after the other, determined not to leave until they were all maxed completely. I didn't need the money. I was just being greedy.

After completing the task, I made my way to the exit. I could see that the others were also headed out. Like normal, we didn't behave as if we knew one another yet we weren't far in proximity. As I reached outside, I could see two uniformed police officers walking past my best friend and her aunt. The officers didn't seem to have any interest in them so I took that as an indication that they weren't here for us. *"Maybe they're just randomly going inside the store for something"* I thought. All of sudden a guy in civilian clothes ran out of the store, shouting while pointing towards us.

"It's those three women" he quickly called out. "I was the one that called. We believe that they are using stolen credit cards." He continued.

Suddenly his words became muffled. I couldn't hear anything else because I was too busy trying to find a way out. There was none. I was in the middle of nowhere and for the first time ever, I was caught red handed. I could feel my heart pounding loudly throughout my body as my hands became sweaty.

The police were on us within seconds and they immediately escorted us back inside of the store. Them, along with who I later found out was a loss prevention officer, led us to a private surveillance room. Immediately they took my wallet that was in my hand. Inside contained all of the credit cards that I just used. *"It's over for me"*

They informed us that we would be held in that room until they were able to figure everything out. I was happy that they allowed us to keep our cell phones since we weren't officially under arrest. I called my man and told him exactly what was happening. He was concerned and worried so he stayed on the phone with me for the entire time.

"Just tell them it was all me. What can they do to me?" He suggested.

"Babe, I'm not going to do that, that's just crazy" I responded.

We ended up sitting in that small room for about three hours as they worked to crack the case. I realized then that they didn't exactly know what we were doing. They only had suspicions about us because of the amount of cards that we were swiping. That gave me a little hope.

We knew better than to tell anything, hoping that they wouldn't be able to figure anything out. Meanwhile, I was praying over and over in my mind like *"Lord, if you get me out of this, I will never swipe another credit card another day in my life."* Little did I know, God had different plans. It took a good while but they did end up figuring it out. Bestie ended up being released because she managed to slip her credit cards inside of her underwear. That stunt she pulled actually saved her.

Unfortunately, myself and her aunt ended up being arrested for credit card fraud. The moment that I felt the cold metal bracelets hit my wrist, I knew it was real. As they were transporting us to the police precinct, her aunt asked questions pertaining to processing expectations. I wasn't cold but I was shivering from fear. We were told that we would most likely be granted a bail in the morning once we were able to see the magistrate. I barely heard anything, as I was in a complete trance the entire time.

I knew that money wasn't an issue for me so if bail was the case then I would be out in no time. Evening was becoming night and I was extremely exhausted and desperately wanting my bed. I wanted this process to go by quickly so that I could pay my way out. I needed to be released as soon as possible to get home to my baby. *"God please fix this"* I silently prayed.

It ended up requiring a lot of string pulling for me to be released. Initially, I was denied bail. Then my guy had to hire an attorney to schedule a bail hearing in order to get me out. The entire process took about a month. Twenty thousand dollars later I was released. Unbeknownst to me, I had much bigger problems.

I never expected my sloppiness to cost me as much as it did. On that day, I unknowingly opened up a can of worms. What I didn't know was that during the previous seven months, NCIS was actively investigating eight of us. They were building extensive case files on each of us. The only piece that they were missing were our identities. My arrest would turn out to be the least of my problems. I handed the feds the missing piece to their puzzle. After being fingerprinted and processed, they were able to identify exactly who I was and that was something that they never knew prior to that day.

"Mealtime!" An officer exclaimed, pulling me back into the present. Shortly after I heard the slot in the door open and a plastic tray became visible. The food resembled dog food but I put salt on it and ate it quickly. Then I washed it down with cold tap water from the sink. It did the job as I no longer felt hunger pains. I made a decision not to allow my circumstances to bother me. Instead of being sad about it, I added it to my list of ammunition. It was only another reason why I would never return to prison.

ALL THINGS COME TOGETHER

A s I mentioned before Philly was a relatively calm facility, and I believe that it was that way because of how anal the administration was. They would lockdown the entire unit, sometimes for several days, for the smallest and pettiest things. This was very annoying to me as an inmate. The consequences were much different than any other facility than I had ever been in. In Philly, Peter always paid for Paul.

As a result of them upholding their no nonsense reputation, they chose to make an example out of me. When my DHO time in the SHU came to an end, I wasn't released back into population. Sammy was released back to the unit while it was decided that I would stay locked in to be transferred out. They determined from the video footage that I was the aggressor, since I went into her cell. Unfortunately they weren't able to find the exact time that she ran in my cell just a day earlier. The decision was unfair, but there was no sense in trying to challenge it. *"Maybe everything happens for a reason"* I thought.

I was hoping to be transferred back to MDC Brooklyn. I really wanted to see my children, and I wanted to be closer to home. Just knowing that I only had one year left in my sentence was enough to give me joy. Instead of being anxious and getting upset, I prayed that this would work out for my benefit.

Once a week, mainline would walk through the SHU corridor, to check on us, just as they did on the regular housing unit. The case manager would walk through with them. I previously requested to be transferred to Brooklyn but was denied because I hadn't been in the facility for a full eighteen months. I prayed that decision would change now that I was being forced to transfer. The case manager assured me that she would do what she could to assist me. I crossed my fingers and prayed that this transfer would work in my favor especially since she took a liking to me.

During those days of uncertainty, I quoted this scripture endlessly *"And we know that all things work together for good to them that love God, to them who are called according to his purpose."* I believed that God was using confusion and contention for my good. Thankfully I ended up being designated to Brooklyn MDC. When the case manager came to tell me the news, I could feel my dry lips split from smiling so widely. I would finally be able to see my kiddos again. There wasn't anything else that could bring me that level of contentment. I laid on my bunk filled with happiness just thinking about it. Years passed since I saw them in person and I couldn't wait to squeeze them.

It did take a few months to get transferred out. The patience that I exercised surprised me as I am naturally an impatient person. I will say that it was time well spent. I was able to sort through many things in my mind that I wouldn't have thought about otherwise. Thankfully I didn't have to get accustomed to a new bunkie while I awaited my transfer. I preferred living alone as I desperately wanted to maintain my peace. Thankfully God's favor was on me. The officers respected my request and left me alone in the cell.

As far as my husband and ex-bestie were concerned, I completely pushed thoughts of them out of my mind. I refused to think about it. My strategy was to be more intentional with my thoughts. Through prayer, reading, exercising, and consistency, I was able to push through sanely. I also held on to the notion that I wouldn't be in Philly much longer and would soon be able to see my children. Nothing was going to jeopardize my positive newfound mindset because I was determined to thrive.

A FULL CIRCLE

I don't think that it was an accident or a coincidence that I was ending my sentence in the same place that I began. I believe that it was symbolic of a full circle. I'm convinced that God had his hand in all of it, even when I stopped praying. I was back in MDC, but I was no longer the same person. I wasn't aware about it then, but prison changed me, and all of those changes weren't for the better.

A few of the girls that I knew were still there fighting their cases. Some were still fighting appeals after all of those years. In addition, many of the girls that were in Danbury were also there carrying out their sentences. They all seemed happy to see me. We spent a lot of time catching up with one another. It was pleasing to know that I was able to inspire change. I discovered that after I was gone, the warden permitted a few women's families to visit them at the hospital after giving birth. It warmed my heart to hear that.

I spoke about all of the drama that I endured along my journey and a lot of the women were surprised. They were also curious about the dynamics of my relationship with my son that I gave birth to when I was there before. I wasn't too sure of how to answer that question. Instead, I shared my pictures with them.

The questions that the ladies asked did inspire the wheels of my mind turn. I realized that I didn't know the answer to a lot of their questions. I would talk to my baby boy on the phone, and he seemed genuinely happy to hear from me, but we only engaged in small talk. Our talks consisted of mostly the same recurring conversation. It was a touchy subject. I realized that I didn't have a close relationship with my baby due to the distance but I was also praying that it would somehow change because I was closer in proximity.

On the contrary, the conversations with my oldest son were more organic. He was surprisingly able to remember a lot of stuff that happened before I left for prison. He was mature for his age. As a result, we had more of a connection than my younger son and I. I desperately wanted to fix that. It was a blessing that my friends were willing to bring both of them to visit me. I was looking forward to having my visiting privileges restored the entire time that I was in transit. Surprisingly my husband also agreed to bring the kids but I wasn't going to hold my breath waiting.

I was able to begin my visits as soon as the case manager cleared my visitation list. For some reason, my suspended visitations didn't transfer with me and obviously I didn't remind them. I appreciated the small miracle, another reflection of God's favor.

My first time visiting with my kids was emotional. My oldest son ran into my arms immediately, and his younger brother followed suit. When we took our seats, I noticed they were inspecting me from head to toe. My younger son repeatedly touched my face while I studied every eye lash and every fingernail of his. I couldn't understand why Aunt K had my baby wearing two side by side ponytails but I knew better than to complain about anything.

I didn't waste my breath because I knew that it would fall on deaf ears. Instead, I made plans to cut his hair as soon as I was released. I would become annoyed when the officers and other visitors referred to him as a girl. Aside from that, I was amazed at how much they had grown. They were handsome, and I couldn't get enough of them. My oldest son asked difficult questions and they caught me off guard every time.

"Mommy, why is everyone wearing the same brown jumper?" He asked filled with curiosity.

"Baby you know that we are here in school. This is our uniform." I said softly.

"So why can't you leave with us.? He persisted.

"Well Mommy isn't quite finished yet, but I will be very very soon." I replied, trying my hardest not to cry.

Those were the best answers that I could come up with. I couldn't bring myself to tell him that I was locked up even though he probably already knew.

With the help of my friends, I was able to see my kids often. My husband also brought them to see me. During those visits, we were cordial and respectful. I was just happy to be able to bond with them, and I refused to be distracted.

My younger son loved to make his way to my lap and lay his head on my chest. He was sweet and loving. At first it was strange because I hadn't felt anything so delicate in such a long time. I had to force myself to become affectionate towards him. I was happy that it didn't take long to make the adjustment. Overall I felt blessed to be able to share those precious moments with my children especially after going so long with seeing them.

I remember trying to prepare myself for resistance from my younger son, prior to them coming to visit me. I thought that he might be a little hesitant to connect with me and I was prepared to give him some space and time to adjust. Thankfully, he was the total opposite. Everything about him was inviting.

As I visited. I couldn't help but repeatedly think of all the women who lost their children to the system while in prison. Though I didn't have the assistance of my family, God kept my children safe until I could care for them personally. I often found myself thanking God for Aunt K. I couldn't wait to get home to them so that I could shower them with the love and attention that they needed. I vowed that once I left prison I was never coming back, and I had two big reasons not to.

One thing about Brooklyn MDC that I despised were the ratchet officers. Thankfully, I programmed my mind to refrain from getting into altercations. I planned to stay to myself as much as possible and bolt at the first sign of drama. Unfortunately for me, I wasn't prepared for the disrespectful officers, and lieutenants. I wasn't accustomed to this level of disrespect from those who were in authority. This new crew of officers were most unprofessional.

I witnessed officers behave in petty ways before but never to the level of antagonizing inmates out of boredom. They usually didn't want to do any paperwork. These officers were different. They seemed to welcome the drama. Most of them were young, new to the job and unprofessional.

Some of the male officers were having inappropriate interactions with the inmates. I knew about it but opted to mind my business. I was too close to the end and I wanted to avoid being caught up in any investigations. Brooklyn MDC didn't have any order. In fact, just two days before I was released, our ghetto fabulous counselor, whom I couldn't stand, had a tantrum. She was upset with my lack of response to her antagonism and ended up pouring a full cup of water on my freshly made bed. She often enjoyed nitpicking but I always refused to respond.

"Now what?" she asked daringly. I only stared at her until she walked away.

Everyone was waiting for a show. Some of the women whom I was previously acquainted with from Danbury expected my temper to get the best of me. What they didn't know is that I was scheduled to be released in two days and planned to walk out peacefully. I choose to keep my release date private to prevent anyone from jeopardizing it. This was a practice that was typical.

The irony of this situation was that it was my counselor who was trying to jeopardize my release. Counselors are more familiar with our cases because they work more closely with us, alongside the case managers. That's why she knew my release date. Even though she held a position of authority, I wasn't surprised by her actions. At this point nothing surprised me. The positive part of it was my being able to recognize my transformation. Sometimes we don't realize how much we have changed, until we are confronted with situations to test us. Our response to those new circumstances is often a good way to measure growth. I was proud of how I chose to handle it.

I didn't say a word, nor did I report her. I didn't want anything to backfire on me, so I held my peace and my tongue. I changed my bed sheets and went on with my day like it never happened. I didn't even allow myself to become angry. My mind was already outside of the prison gates. I had laser beam focus and immediately weighed my options. Thankfully I knew better than to allow a fat, short, ghetto, hazel contact lense wearing officer to get in the way of my freedom. The only thing that I could think about were the two kids that were waiting for me.

THE DAY THAT I PRAYED FOR

For those that were scheduled to be released, at 6 a.m. sharp, the officer on duty would tap the rail of their beds with keys. That was our alarm clock. Those inmates would be informed that they were on the release roster. They would also be granted early access to the showers before everyone woke up for breakfast. I was different from the others. I didn't need a wake up call.

On that day, I woke up at 5 a.m. sharp. Even though I only had the opportunity to sleep for three hours, I wasn't tired at all. In fact I had more energy than ever. After counting down for the last sixty-days, it was surreal to finally be down to the last few hours. I continuously pinched myself to ensure that it was real.

I have spurs in my memory regarding this day. A lot of time was spent sitting at a table in the common area waiting to be called to R and D. I listened to my MP3 player and patiently waited. *"I'm actually going to R and D to be discharged"* I thought. Each time that I previously went through receiving and discharge it was because I was being received by an institution. This time around, I was being discharged.

I was proud of myself. I know that may seem bizarre, but it was an exhilarating feeling making it to the finish line. I kept thinking, *"wow I really did it. I made it and I'm still me. I'm still a good person. This time didn't turn me into a monster."* I knew that I was still capable of being loving and kind and I was grateful for that. I was in a good space mentally and that meant everything to me.

Although I was in a stage of healing, I was still unaware of how damaged I actually was. I strongly believe that if one is unaware of how damaged they are, it is impossible to move forward with true healing. Untreated trauma is similar to untreated cancer. If it isn't completely addressed then it becomes detrimental. I was dangerously unaware of the amount of trauma that my incarceration experience inflicted.

As I was seated comfortably in the common area with my headphones on, my mind swirled with numerous random thoughts. *"Even if it takes all day, they must release me. It would be illegal for them to keep me beyond today."* I found irony in the fact that I was in a rush to get to a unit when I came in, yet I wasn't in a rush to be released.

As I waited, I began to reflect on my time away. My progress was obvious and I appreciated that. Everyone that knew me in the beginning of serving my time, went out of their way to tell me that they could see my growth. Even the woman Vee that I had a fight with as a result of gambling, gave me my flowers. She was one of the women who were transferred to MDC when Danbury forced us out. We didn't end up being friends again but we were respectful to one another and cordial.

I made huge strides to improve my life and I knew that it was vital for me to continue in that direction. It is important to continue growing because there isn't ever a true destination. We are all on a journey. It's just that some of our journeys are more horrifying than others. The bible says that God doesn't give us more than we can bear. I guess that's why some of us are given a heavier load. We are the soldiers.

I thought that leaving prison was the end of my horror movie, but it was only the beginning of part two. I was clueless about what my future entailed but that didn't matter because I told myself that no matter what, it couldn't be worse than how I'd spent the previous five years. Confidence and faith are always good but I lacked a concrete plan as to where I was headed in my next season.

James 2:14 *"What does it profit, my brethren, if someone says he has faith but does not have works? Can faith save him?"*

Apart from that, I was thankful that there was a box containing civilian clothes waiting for me in R and D. I didn't want to be one of those women who left prison in a commissary issued sweatsuit. I wanted to leave everything behind. The facility allows clothes to be sent in a few weeks prior to release. Thankfully, my friend Dee, the one that told me about my husband's affair, did the honors of showing up for me. Unfortunately, I didn't get to see what she sent in. Honestly I didn't care. I was only hoping that I estimated my size correctly. After years of wearing mostly sweats, it was hard for me to estimate my size.

I was wondering how many people would be waiting on the opposite side of the gate for me. I felt horrible that they all were waiting for so long. I was sure my husband and my kids would be there even though we weren't on the best of terms. He let me down, yes but I knew he would show up on my release day. Though we were no longer together, he was decent enough to make sure that I had a ride. He knew that I had no contact with my family, so I was sure that he would come through.

Riding with him would be somewhat awkward, but I was hoping that we could utilize the ride to talk things over. I was due to report to the halfway house within a few hours of release where I would be receiving an ankle monitor. After a few hours, I would then be on my way to Aunt K's place. I wasn't sure if I wanted to rekindle our relationship, but I knew that I wanted to be cool for the sake of the kids.

As we all know, time moves much quicker when we aren't obsessively checking in on it. Hours passed as I became lost in thought and before I knew it, I was in R and D changing into my civilian clothes. I was grateful that they fit me perfectly. Strangely, I don't remember the long walk from the unit to the changing room in R and D. In my mind, I was already on the opposite side of the gate.

I can recall suddenly feeling excited once I finished changing. It was at that moment, my release became real to me. One of the girls that I grew close to was also being released on the same day that I was. She and I shared our anticipation and excitement with one another. She also changed. Together we took a moment to soak in the reality of wearing real clothing.

"I can't believe it's over, I just want to hug my daughter," she said to me. Those words echoed in my mind. They confirmed our new status. I'd certainly take being a felon over being an inmate any day.

"It's really over" I thought.

As the officer escorted us to the gate, the sun instantaneously bathed my face. I hadn't experienced direct sunlight in a long time, so I enjoyed the beaming sun rays. It was a bit chilly outside, but I didn't care. I appreciated the fresh wind cutting me. It was better than the stuffy recycled air. I inhaled deeply as I watched the gate sliding open, I could hear my heart pounding hard inside of my chest. I didn't know what I was feeling but I knew that it had to be good.

"Don't come back," the escorting officer said casually, as if he had said it a million times before. My friend and I both laughed, and we both confirmed that wasn't an option.

As I was walking out, I was careful not to look back. There is this superstition amongst inmates, in prison, that forbids us from turning around and looking back at the prison after we are released. It is said that if we look back at any point as we are being released, then we will likely return. I made sure to keep my focus forward as I walked.

Although superstitions conflict with Christianity, I wasn't interested in testing out the accuracy. I didn't know what lied ahead, but the one thing that I did know without a shadow of a doubt, was that I was never going to come back to a federal prison.

Walking to the curb, my eyes danced wildly looking out to see who was there waiting for me. The further that I walked onto the sidewalk, the more I could feel anxiety filling my body. I was hypersensitive to everything happening and it was beginning to feel overwhelming.

Suddenly, the ground began trembling beneath me. I froze. *"Is this an earthquake?"* I thought to myself. I scanned my surroundings and quickly realized that there was a truck speeding in my direction. Impulsively, I jumped back further onto the sidewalk. Once the truck passed, I began to analyze the situation and quickly realized that the truck was nowhere near the curb. I couldn't help but think, *"Why did I react that way? Why did I jump back?"* This was one of my first indications that something might be wrong.

After that, I heard an unfamiliar voice calling my name. The person calling my name can be described as a middle aged, dark skinned, west indian man. He had a salt and pepper beard and was tall in stature. He didn't look familiar to me but I couldn't help but notice that he was fine. Looking past him, I began to search for a more familiar face. I knew that my husband had to be out there somewhere. *"Did he really leave me high and dry like this?"*

The guy called out to me again and I slowly walked towards him. When I was in closer proximity to him, he began to explain that a friend of mine sent him because she had to work and couldn't be there. He informed me that he was her father. He also explained that he wanted to leave some time ago but decided to wait because he was aware that no one else was coming to pick me up. I was uncomfortable that a stranger felt sorry for me. I was also curious as to why he seemed to know more than I did. After a few moments of additional confirmation, I decided to believe his story.

My friend who was released alongside me, couldn't find her family and asked to use the guy's cell phone. After confirming that her family was closeby, he offered to take her to them as they had gotten lost on the way to the institution. I was much more comfortable with the two of us riding with him, than just me alone. It gave me extra time to check his vibe. Together we made small talk and rode along until we met up with her family.

I was only half engaged in the conversation happening in the car. I was more so in my own head. It was disappointing that my husband hadn't sent anyone to pick me up. *"Wow he really doesn't care about me anymore"* I thought. Although he continuously showed signs of who he really was, something in me continued to be hopeful. Unfortunately my hopefulness caused me to be more disappointed each time. I was hurt all over again due to forming my own expectations. *"Am I really on my own?"* I thought, trying hard not to believe it. Soon after we dropped my friend off to her family.

Unfamiliarity conjures up skepticism and skeptical about this man I was. I was looking for someone familiar after serving my time and disappointed when I saw none. I believe that this is one of the key reasons as to why people often fall back into the same traps after being released. We often search for familiarity when it's not in our best interest. God knew what was best for me even though I wasn't able to recognize it. I learned through this experience, that what is best, often feels uncomfortable.

As we navigated through Brooklyn, I noticed that everyone was dolled up and beautiful as if they were on television. This prompted me to look at myself in the passenger side mirror. I was disappointed at the reflection that was staring back at me. I could no longer see my beauty.

"Can we make a quick stop to Sephora?" I asked.

My friend's dad was nice enough to oblige. I already knew what foundation I wanted to purchase. In my pocket were pictures from magazines of items that I wanted. I only had a few dollars to my name, but I needed makeup desperately. I couldn't wait. There was no way that I could allow anyone to see me with these dark marks on my face. That harsh prison water certainly did a number on my skin but I planned to fix that as soon as possible.

Sephora was close in distance so it didn't take long for us to arrive. As I walked in, I became overwhelmed by all the bright lights. I previously visited the same location and I could see that everything was completely different. It caught me by surprise.

"Can I help you?" A saleswoman asked me as soon as I walked in.

"Yes please, I need something to cover all of this up" I said while pointing to my face. "I don't have much time," I added.

"Ok no problem. Do you have a particular brand in mind?" she continued.

"Yes, something like this." I said while handing her a magazine ad that I pulled out of my pocket.

The area between the saleswoman's eyebrows crinkled, and I could tell that she was curious about me. Feelings of shame consumed me as I looked to the floor. Before I knew it, she had the makeup in hand and was asking if she could test to see if the color matched my complexion. Then she proceeded to explain the product, while sponging the tester onto the side of my face. After she was finished, she held up a mirror in front of my face. I couldn't have been more disappointed with what appeared before me.

I hated what I was seeing. The bright lights in the store only amplified what I originally saw in the car mirror. I could see that my skin aged significantly and my pores were visible. I had dark marks throughout and overall I looked dull. The only part of my face that was appealing was the small area where the foundation was applied.

"I'll take it," I said quickly. "Also can you please apply this to my entire face?" I asked. I didn't want to look at my real skin any longer.

"Sure," She replied warmly.

Soon after, I was back in the car and we were on our way. Before dropping me off at the halfway house, my friend's dad asked me if I was hungry. When I admitted that I was, he pulled up to Juniors Restaurant located downtown Brooklyn. I looked at the menu, then ordered what I saw was least expensive.

As I waited for my take out, all I could think about was how much the world changed. Initially, I thought that leaving prison would be the best feeling in the world. Unfortunately that only lasted for a few moments. Now that I was free, worry, panic and stress set in. I didn't have a game plan, and I now knew that I was in this world all alone. Everything that I once had was all gone. I only invested in material items therefore I didn't have anything that was of any real value. My jewelry and my designer pieces were all stolen. My marriage was in shambles and I barely knew my children. I was stripped of everything, including my identity. My new title was ex-convict.

Not only was I stripped but I also owed every dime that I stole through my schemes. With only the clothes on my back to my name, it finally dawned on me. I had a host of regrets. None of this was worth it and it took almost five years for me to figure that out. *"It was all for nothing"* I thought. I could feel my hands becoming clammy as my reality hit home. *"What else am I going to do besides fail again?"* My thoughts were scattered. I couldn't even focus long enough to pray. This was the moment where I began to realize that I was preparing to embark on part two of my troubles. I was no longer A Black Girl in Orange. I was now A Black Girl Lost.

End of book one

Bonus Chapter

:::

THE WOMEN INSIDE

As human beings we all desire some level of connection. My detachment from the free world pushed me to connect with the women on the inside. I found out that all of the women weren't bad. In fact, I learned that everyone has some good in them, even if they have done horrible things.

I met some of the most talented and intelligent women on the planet, behind the wall. The women I met didn't allow their circumstances to prevent them from being creative. I admired how they made an effort to celebrate and entertain one another. They would throw birthday parties, barbecues, fashion shows and even create stage plays that were better than the ones created by Tyler Perry. On the flipside of what was negative, I was able to see the beauty and talent of women.

The saying "hurt people, hurt people" couldn't be more true. The more that I became acquainted with the women inside was the more that I was able to understand why we were hurtful towards one another. We were all broken and enduring turbulent times together just like one big family. I have never heard of a family that didn't experience some level of hurt amongst one another.

Behind the wall there was no shortage of personality. In fact, you could get a good laugh just by taking a walk outside on the compound and eavesdropping on a few conversations. The federal system is filled with people from around the world. At every turn you could hear a different accent. Somehow, even under such sad circumstances, I was fond of the beautiful diversity.

Many miracles also took place behind the wall. I have witnessed the release of women who shouldn't have seen the light of day. I knew in my heart that their release was nothing other than the power of God. Witnessing such honor always brought tears to my eyes. It was remarkable to witness the impossible becoming possible.

While in prison I met a wonderful woman named Ramona Brant. Ms. Ramona, as I called her, was an honorable woman who was serving a life sentence for a drug conspiracy case. She is one person who I believe was truly innocent. Prior to being committed to prison, she was a victim of domestic violence, who suffered at the hands of her children's father. I learned through conversing with her that he was a major drug dealer in their community. She attested that she never participated in any of his business activities, and there was very little evidence against her, yet the court found her guilty anyway. Her case is an example of how the system could be cruel to those who were often the real victims.

Ms. Ramona was a shining example of faith. We met during a mandatory orientation upon my arrival to Danbury. She was one of three model inmates that spoke to the newly sentenced inmates committed to the facility. She was considered to be a model inmate because she never received any disciplinary action during her incarceration. I believe that God used her to speak to me as she was a devoted Christian who saved many souls behind the wall. I noticed that she was always gracious despite her circumstances. I was truly able to see God within her.

I once spoke to her about her life-long sentence and with great conviction she reassured me that she would not die in prison. At that moment, I held my tongue because I didn't want to share my disbelief. My faith wasn't strong enough to believe that her sentence could be overturned. After all, she had gone through several lengthy appeals and received the same results each time. Despite the odds being stacked against her, Ms. Ramona never allowed herself to lose hope or faith in God.

She shared with me that she had a calling on her life for prison ministry. She often said she was there to minister and save souls that no one else had the capacity to reach. I witnessed her apply for clemency only to be denied but Ms. Ramona didn't allow that to deter her faith. Shortly after that denial, she boldly began to give all of her belongings away.

With great faith, I heard her declare. "I'll be in the next round. I know that I am about to be released."

I thought for sure that my prison mentor was losing her mind. With my natural eyes I couldn't foresee what she was seeing in the spiritual realm. I am slightly ashamed to admit that I didn't believe that she would ever be free.

One afternoon in MDC Brooklyn, our unit was visited by a group of prison administrators. When everyone was assembled, they made a huge announcement. They told Ms. Ramona that she was granted clemency from President Obama. I couldn't believe my ears as my mouth hung open. I witnessed a miracle firsthand. Ms. Ramona was a living testament of God's grace and favor. This was a joyous moment for us all.

I saw her leap for joy and I knew firsthand that this news was confirmation of what she confessed with her mouth all along. During her last days in prison, I stuck to her like glue. I wanted to be connected to the power that was within her. On the day of her release, I was proudly standing beside her as she exited the unit at five am to be received by press, family, and friends. I ended up being released shortly after. I can recall speaking with her when I got out. It was then that I learned that she was blessed with the opportunity to have lunch with President Barack Obama at the White House.

"Girl, I went from sleeping on a hard prison cot for over twenty years, to gaining the honor of having lunch with the president of the

United States of America. If that isn't God's favor then I don't know what is." She told me.

I felt her powerful words vibrate in my soul. That day we spoke on the phone for over an hour. Not much longer after that conversation, I learned of Ms. Ramona's death. I was immensely saddened and I felt as if she was cheated out of a full life. I felt she didn't have the opportunity to experience freedom properly.

Her promise to me was that she wouldn't die in prison. Although her life was short lived, it was a beautiful example of God's omnipotent power. Her kind and gentle spirit was what ultimately led me back to my faith. For these reasons, I can never forget her.

Many of my prison sisters have been released and gone on to do great things. A host of them own and operate thriving businesses. Some have become best-selling authors and much more. I admire how we are able to utilize our lemons to produce tasty lemonade. Although our experiences were unpleasant, we recognize the purpose in it, which is why we choose to inspire multitudes through our stories.

Even despite these strides, the stigma of incarceration remains. We are often scrutinized and judged because of our former choices. These days I am proud to be a part of this population. My life is a shining example that conveys; a checkered past has nothing to do with having a glorious future. It is common knowledge that the highest amount of pressure produces diamonds. I like to view myself, along with others who were and still are incarcerated, as coal. The pressure was simply a tool to refine us.

SNEAK PEEK OF BOOK TWO

I can recall feeling hopeful. My husband was treating me well and I was on the verge of falling for him again. I enjoyed the fact that he would visit me often as he was aware that I couldn't move around freely, due to my ankle monitor. When he wasn't visiting me, he would call to check on me numerous times throughout the day. Anything that I asked for, he went out of his way to provide. *"Girl, he still loves you. You better get him back. Besides, who else is going to want you with two kids?"* I thought. As more of this continued, I became open to the idea of becoming a family again.

At the same time, I was trying hard not to think about my old best friend. That was difficult because she was living in the adjacent building from where I was staying. I would literally be looking out of the window and see her son playing outside along with other members of their family. Everything around me reminded me of her, including my husband. A lot of times, he would join me at Aunt K's house and stay with me for majority of the day. During those hours, I was filled with contentment however when it came time for him to leave at night, I immediately became upset. I knew that he was going home to her and I just couldn't stomach it.

Daily, my emotions went up and down like a seesaw. I would plummet from experiencing extreme happiness to feeling extreme despair. Once he left at night, I couldn't fall asleep. I would be too occupied with envisioning the two of them cuddled together and having sex. Uncontrollable thoughts would creep into my mind of me severely hurting my old friend. These thoughts would often be followed by a prayer asking God to change my thinking but God was taking his time. I truly didn't want to be that vengeful person yet I couldn't seem to get past my brokenness no matter how hard I tried.

On one occasion, as I laid in a complete rage, I lost control. I decided that I was going to find her. It didn't matter to me that my whereabouts were being tracked through my ankle monitor. I planned to cross that bridge when I got to it. I decided that I wasn't going to lay in turmoil, wondering what my husband and her were doing. Instead I would go and find out. Impulsively, I sprung up and before I knew it, I was on my way to her apartment door.

When I slipped out, I purposely didn't tell Aunt K that I was leaving because I didn't want her to stop me. I felt as if I were having an out of body experience and I was truly unable to control myself. Thoughts of hurting my old friend consumed me. All I wanted was for her to pay for everything that I was feeling. I desperately wanted her to hurt like I was hurting.

I proceeded to knock on her apartment door loudly. When no one answered, I began yelling obscenities in an effort to force her to come out. Then I began kicking the door. Finally, her older male cousin opened it. I attempted to peer around him while aggressively yelling for her to come out. I could hardly hear anything that he was saying because I was completely in a rage. I could see her son peeking at me but I didn't care. I began to perspire as my blood pressure rose.

"She's not here Tee, I swear" Her cousin told me in an attempt to get me to leave. "She just left for a concert going on in the Barclay Center" He continued.

"Yea sure" I replied in a tone that told him I didn't believe him.

Before he could see it coming, I punched him in his face hard. "Hold that for her then." I told him before walking off to press the elevator button. I looked back to see him covering his lip with his hand. Soon after, I was back at Aunt K's house like nothing happened. After sipping a bit of her wine, I proceeded to lay down on the top bunk still seething. My baby son climbed in bed to join me, leaning his head on my chest like always. *"I'm just gonna catch her the next time"* I thought as I dozed off hugging my precious baby.

147

Made in the USA
Middletown, DE
26 June 2023

33737651R00089